Secrets Revealed for EXTRAORDINARY Success

Change of Approach, a fantastic life-changing guide for faster Personal & Professional growth

Secrets Revealed for EXTRAORDINARY Success

Change of Approach, a fantastic life-changing guide for faster Personal & Professional growth

Authored by

Shivali Tandon

WINGS PUBLICATION

WE GIVE WINGS TO YOUR DREAM!

Disclaimer

WINGS PUBLICATION
WE GIVE WINGS TO YOUR DREAM!

Registered Office- 907-Sneh Nagar, Sapna Sangeeta Road,
Agrasen Square, Indore – 452001 (M.P.), India
Website: http://www.wingspublication.com
Email: mybook@wingspublication.com

First Published by WINGS PUBLICATION 2021

Title: Secrets Revealed! for Extraordinary Success
Price: INR 599 /$ 14.99

ISBN 978-93-90661-03-9

LIMITS OF LIABILITY/DISCLAIMER OF WARRANTY

The Author of this book is solely responsible and liable for its content including but not limited to the views, representations, descriptions, statements, information, opinions and references. The information presented in this book is solely compiled by the Author from sources believed to be accurate and the Publisher assumes no responsibility for any errors or omissions. The information is not intended to replace or substitute professional advice.

The Content of this book shall not constitute or be construed or deemed to reflect the opinion or expression of the Publisher. Publisher of this book does not endorse or approve any content of this book or guarantee the reliability, accuracy or completeness of the content published herein and do not make any representations or warranties of any kind, express or implied, including but not limited to the implied warranties of merchantability, fitness for a particular purpose. The Publisher shall not be held liable whatsoever for any errors, omissions, whether such errors or omissions result from negligence, accident, or any other cause or claims for loss or damages of any kind, including without limitation, indirect or consequential loss or damage arising out of use, inability to use, or about the reliability, accuracy or sufficiency of the information contained in this book. All disputes are subject to Indore (M.P.) jurisdiction only.

Author's Disclaimer

"The names, characters, professions, businesses, places, events, and incidents are just the author's imagination or used in a fictitious manner to create various scenarios in this book. Any resemblance to actual persons, living or dead, or actual events is purely coincidental."

Dedicated to...

To my mother & my loving husband, they have always encouraged me to do something great in life. They are my strength, and it would not have been possible without their support.

Acknowledgement

Words will fall short of saying thank you to the "Creator" of this Universe who is always with me, inside my heart. Thank you for showing me this path. I know you exist in each one of us.

I would like to thank the one and only person who is next to God for me and because of her, I am who I am. She is my world, My Mom! Thank you, maa... I love you from the bottom of my heart and you are the reason I see dreams and work hard to turn them into reality!

I would like to thank the most important person of my life, my best friend, my better half, my strength, and my life, thank you Mr. Husband, you know this is for you! Without your support and encouragement, this was impossible. Your unconditional love for me is a blessing that I have received from God. Thanks, from the bottom of my heart!

I am more than happy to say a big thanks to my two wonderful families, Tandons & Kashyaps, who have always supported me to achieve my goals. I love you all!

Thanks to my two munchkin heartbeats Atharv & Mridul for filling my life with love & just the love…

Deepest gratitude and love for my father, who is not with us, but I know he is always watching me & protecting me from above.

Special thanks to the mentors & guides who have directly or indirectly inspired from a far distance, Dr. Daisaku Ikeda, Shri Sadhguru ji, Tony Robbins, Vivek Bindra, Oprah Winfrey; their life experiences & guidance has made it easy for me to believe in myself. Deepest gratitude & thanks to Kailash Pinjani Sir who guided me through to make this dream come true.

Thanks to my dear friends for their blessings & support. Special thanks to Lokesh and Praveen for helping me shape up this book.

Immense gratitude for Aanchal, Kavita ji and Jayanti aunty who selflessly had supported me during hard times with their prayers.

I am deeply thankful to each one of you who have been a part of my life and reading this and even if I have not mentioned your names, my gratitude will surely reach to you through cosmos energies. I love you all! Thanks.

Preface

This book is very special to me as I have penned down the best of the Principles, rules & mantras that were & are part of my "Change of Approach" journey. I found a way to change life for the better each day, and I found this word **"change"** so impactful that I was forced to pen it down for you all.

In this book, you will find real-time illustrations of the problems we face at work that hinder our growth as a working professional and how it impacts our personal life. At the end of the book after inculcating these 18 success principles, you will surely change your approach as a **Top Performer at your workplace that ultimately guarantees a prosperous personal life.** Consider this **'change of approach'** not as a strategy but as a "process".

Learning for me is to experience the phase we are into at present; I have not picked up these Principles from anywhere, but these are the extracts of what I have experienced so far and with this my Change of Approach journey goes on & on... It is more special for me as I am working as an associate and as an HR professional both, this has really helped me to showcase both sides of the coin from the organisational side as well the side of an associate. I have seen most people fail because they do not have a clear vision; they do not know the type of work that makes them happy; they do not know the purpose of their life.

You will notice three major things in the book: Proactive Approaches, Models/illustrations for real-time application and lastly activities that will help you find your weaknesses & strengths.

On this journey of changing your approach towards many things, you will also witness a lot many hypothetical situations and I want you to imagine yourself into each one of them. Ask yourself questions about "*what if I would have been in this scenario or the situation*". This is what I call the perfect way to introspect yourself and your surroundings to find out your strengths as well as weaknesses.

Now with me just imagine hypothetically that when you are trying to dig into the ground beneath your feet, you find some vegetables at first, then some fruits, then when you go lower into the ground it carries some more elements, that makes you feel little better, you did not stop there and dig more deep into the ground & see that it has a layer where there is silver deposits & the more deeper you go into this ground you find gold then diamonds and then some amazing emotions wrapped under another **deepest layer** that is **"Peace", "Happiness"** and the **"Abundance"**, Wow! These fruits, vegetables, the silver, gold, and diamonds are just ways to depict the value of benefits or rewards we get while we are working hard to dig into the ground. But how many of us in actual reach to the core of the ground? How many of us actually are able to dig-in this deep for our Goals that we get to find abundance, financial stability, stable career, ample opportunities and growth in life.

Let us learn my Rule of 24 meters down in 24 hours!

The first 9 meters may have these fruits & vegetables. Maybe initially some of you were satisfied with these benefits, but now that you are reading this book, I am sure your hunger has increased, you are no longer feeling completely satisfied with these first 9 meters of digging under the ground. What if you never ever noticed this fact that with correct focus & hard work on these first 9 to 10 hours of digging, and without getting distracted due to the small benefits & fruits we get on our way, the next 15 meters of digging will be easy and will be much more productive. By using all your skills & strategies, these next 15 meters will become an experience of happiness, peace, mental satisfaction, stable career, limitless opportunities & abundance for you. Come with me & learn how to dig in hard but smartly into the first 9 meters of the ground, i.e., to apply all these 18 success principles during the first 9 hours (let us consider that in 1 hour you cover 1 meter) of work so that rest of the 15 meters (next 15 hours of a day) will become an experience to you & a result of the efforts you had put during these 9 hours of the day!

Proactive Approach: 1

Rule of 24 meters down in 24 hours!

- Digging Deep to find our highest potential -

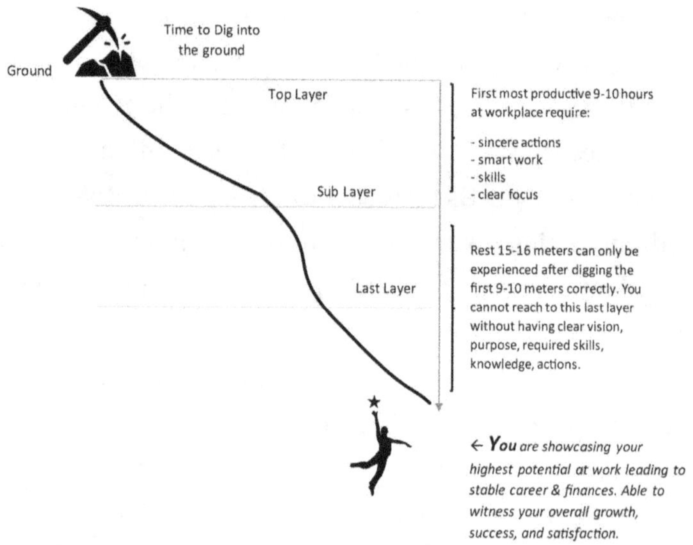

Let us find out the correct approach for getting to the core of this ground. Let us correctly understand the expectations of the current industry & your organisation.

This book will also be perfect for those who are about to make a maiden stint in any industry, even if currently you do not have any exposure to corporate challenges, this guide will help you to have a **Proactive approach,** you will **be all set to showcase your highest potential at work.** I personally feel those who have these "approaches" inculcated in their habits & behaviour well in advance from the beginning of their first job will **see their Career growth graph rise high**

in no time; these associates are more focussed & clearer about their goals from day 1 be it any industry or workplace.

This book that I am calling a guide for my readers will help them to Introspect the "Self", Analyse "Others", Get the "Vision", set up the "Target" & Activate the "Action Mode". That is why I call it a journey of ***change in your approach***. Your targets & vision should be at the same level so that you are not at all distracted in between your career roadmap. Always keep "others" one step ahead of you, respecting them for their potential & skills, always be ready to learn from people around you and then after analysing the requirements in yourself, you take the leap directly towards your goal.

Proactive Approach: 2

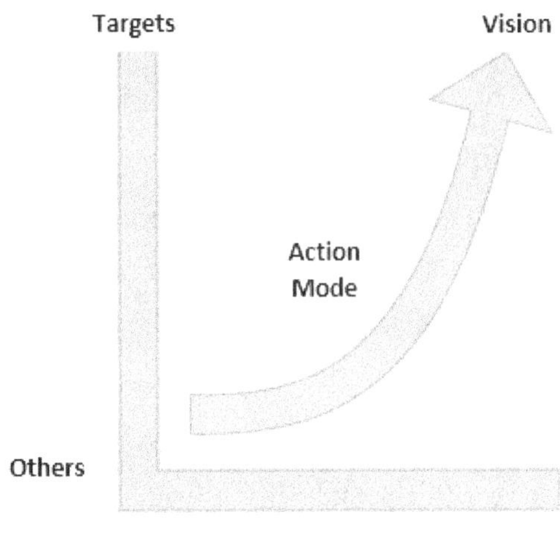

- Activate the Action Mode -

This small word "CHANGE" is so powerful and so

massive that it has the capacity to turn your world upside down, i.e., from Zero to Hero phase!

These Rules and Principles are not for those who only believe in this term "ACTION" but for those of us who are ready to **CHANGE & IMPLEMENT** the required **ACTIONS**. If you really want to become a top performer at your workplace & in your personal life, you must embrace this word **"CHANGE"**, but we have to be very careful that we **do it correctly** because any change that is done by you is invalid if it is not executed with a correct approach.

Follow these 18 Success principles & you will be able to immediately see yourself at the right place where you are more valued, at the place where you are fully skilled & are required in the industry you are working currently. People may have noticed & read about so many solutions, but it really does not matter at all what solution you have applied. What matters is the END RESULT which literally depends upon **HOW we apply the solution** in real-life situations.

So, while you read this book & start understanding the solutions & ideas mentioned in each section, please stick to this phrase "HOW TO APPLY". All your success & transformation depends on this HOW!

This book does not talk about how to get up on time, practice yoga, or try to stay calm for 9 hours at work etc. etc. This book is for those who have the courage to change their overall "APPROACH" and thought process.

Do you know one secret here?? **Every one of us has this COURAGE to change for the better, but only a few can tap this courage from within.**

So, it's time to start this journey together... The journey of change of approach by understanding deeply & correctly about these 18 success principles.

Let's Connect!

"Together we can inspire & can create extraordinary experiences".

Connect directly with the Author...

Facebook:
https://www.facebook.com/ExtraordinaryLife365

YouTube:
https://www.youtube.com/c/ExtraordinaryLife365

LinkedIn:
https://www.linkedin.com/in/shivali-tandon-perseverant/

Instagram:
https://www.instagram.com/extraordinarylife.365/

Email:
extraordinarylife365@gmail.com

Content

Chapter - 1

Problem Areas & where are we?

As you just noticed, this book's Index has only 2 Chapters, yes only 2 chapters. It sounds strange to you?? I agree, it does sound odd to most of the readers but trust me I don't want you to read this book by going through the INDEX TOPICS one after the other to see if anyone or two success principles are applicable to you or not. I want you to go through each success principle and **create your own extraordinary experience.**

The first chapter talks about the problems because of which you would like to read this book & would want to find your highest potential! Also, it has a small reality check about where we are right now!

The 2nd chapter has all the SOLUTIONS, i.e., the 18 success principles that we need to learn and see how to apply these principles correctly to get to the transformation stage!

"If I had an hour to solve a problem, I'd spend 55 minutes thinking about the problem and 5 minutes thinking about solutions."

- Albert Einstein

Many of us, while reading a book, will have this feeling that we have never faced such a problem, so let's skip this topic! My question to my readers is that – what guarantees that this problem will not arise in the near future, as we are advancing technology-wise, skills-wise, socially & globally and the time of PRESENT demands PRE-PREPS, i.e., to have a PROACTIVE approach to face any problem or challenge at work or in our personal life.

So, when you read this book, make sure you keep in mind the complete chain of these 18 success principles that are a whole package to learn! That means not a single topic has to be avoided or ignored even if it may not be related to you at this point of time, as I am sure anybody can encounter these anytime in future.

We sometimes read & read the book, relate ourselves with the problem areas & feel so satisfied & happy that *"oh! that is the issue I am also facing!"*

We start to feel that finally, someone else does understand what we felt or are feeling! Sadly, that spark of focusing upon the solution eliminates gradually! **CHANGE of APPROACH** is thinking broadly & to think a step ahead! To be a problem solver rather than a person who relates himself/herself with the problems and who just sits sad and takes NO ACTION!

No! that's really not going to help!

For this let's do a small activity, a very simple one!

Say aloud this to yourself 3 times:

"I am going to SOLVE all my problems & will take ACTIONS as I am now a Problem solver! I believe in myself. I will make NO EXCUSES from now!"

Common! What are you thinking? Say it please ☺ 3 times.

Thank you for saying it out loud with me 3 times! Yes, as you believe in yourself, I assure you that I also believe in you.

It is very important to clearly understand the problem & weak areas first to find the correct solution. Even if you do not have a problem, you can simply keep these basic problem areas in mind to apply the solutions with the help of these principles, scenarios & action points mentioned in this book. I have tried to cover all major aspects in the book that directly or indirectly affect the associate's performance, growth & success in life! A few may do not even have a problem as mentioned below, but as soon as you turn the pages of the book, you will understand what is stopping you from becoming the best performer at your workplace and how you can find your highest potential in life.

- What if you are working for more than 4 to 5 years in the same organisation but you are still at same Job Level or position, or you are eagerly waiting for a promotion, but your leaders are not even thinking about it?
- You are bored with the same monotonous task, repeated schedules, same reports, same meetings, nothing new to learn at your current workplace?
- Simply looking for growth at work because you have lost motivation, have already put so many efforts but nothing is working in your favour.
- So much of politics around you, manipulative associates around

that you are unable to handle the situation?

- You think there is a lot of favouritism in your team; you are not getting the correct opportunity to express your achieved targets?
- You are not satisfied with the salary & perks, or you are not happy with the average hike given to you, not because it was the standard hike distribution among the associates, but because your manager told you that you need to perform well, and you think you are already performing well in your job?
- Too much work assigned to you & your Manager is still expecting a lot, work pressure is unbearable for you, even after working so hard you are not getting any reward or recognition?
- You are confused about what Type of Work you really like? Or you know already but at your current position whatever work you have, does not make you happy anymore? You are doing your job just because of some circumstances of life. You no longer enjoy the work you do daily?
- You have lost your confidence, or you really don't believe that you can ever be successful like others around you?
- Contradictory to the above one, overconfident but the result still not visible to you! Why?

Let us take a pause for just 2 minutes & introspect ourselves, you have surely understood some basic problems & are able to relate yourself to 1 or more problems. It is really a very good sign if you can understand any 1 or all of these and many more problems like these that impact your growth! Be assured that you will reverse the situation but be ready, to be honest with yourself & be ready to activate your **"Action Mode"**.

I realised that there was a time when people used to show their degrees with high scores at the Job interviews & that is it! They were hired.

As the trend has changed drastically in the last 2 decades that only a degree cannot help. We have a more interactive approach; we are focussed more on the presentation of our associates in front of the stakeholders, clients & end-users. It is all about building a strong base, to have a **"No chance for Error approach"** as there is a lot of competition in the market. What we think now has already been implemented somewhere else! So many sharp intelligent & like-minded people are working together to change the trends day after day, month after month & year after year. We must keep running to match up with the latest trend & techniques.

Yes, of course, the degree does matter, how can anybody ignore "education" which is the first brick of our foundation, but no matter how strong our foundation is, the interiors & the outer presentation also matters! None of these can be compromised. You need both, to have a strong base of the building & at the same time to have the best interior & exteriors of the building which I call **the presentation.** Imagine your career as this building; you have to start thinking about the CORE of it. That first brick, the base you have, i.e., education, qualification, or degree. Trends may have changed but who said the "CORE" had lost its value! *Naaahhh!* It is only like we keep on designing, re-designing the interiors & exteriors of our career.!

So, the first thing we understood here is that we have to focus on both – **our education & our presentation. The presentation** is huge for me; it includes everything starting from the behaviour,

our attitude towards the work, our relationships with colleagues, stakeholders, clients etc., our overall personality, our overall conduct in the real world and ultimately **our APPROACH!** If you compromise with any one of these two important requirements, then you will lose the race!

Don't worry you do not have to stress yourself thinking about the BASE, which you think is not very strong in your case or vice versa you have a strong base, but the presentation is missing! We must understand that there is no age limit for learning, to change for the better, for exploring something new, for trying something new, for starting from "this day" onwards! You have already taken a STEP towards the change you want to see in yourself. You are already reading the book on "this day" which clearly tells that you are ready to accept changes! You are ready to remove all those obstacles that are restricting your growth & success in life. For me, a single step is worth a journey if taken each day consistently.

- Activity: A -

If I say that 10 is the highest score, i.e. showcasing the highest potential at work or consider 10 being the best rating for the upcoming scenario and 1 is the lowest score, then what scores will you give here?

You can do this with a pen & paper, or directly in your mind after reading questions one by one or by writing your answers in your mobile notes; it is up to you how you would like to perform this activity. Don't worry; you can be completely honest with yourself as nobody is going to ask you about the answers. We can do this exercise every week or monthly, just like a reality check for ourselves. This will help us to understand where we stand today & where we must reach in actual. (If you completely agree then 10 will be your score & if you do not agree or are not satisfied then 1 will be your score)

Q1. Are you completely satisfied with your current job?

Score ----------

Q2. How good is the bond between you & your manager?

Score ----------

Q3. How creative are you at your work?

Score ----------

Q4. Do you perform well even when you are under a lot of work pressure?

Score ----------

Q.5. You usually say "yes" to any new task or miscellaneous assignments assigned to you, no matter whether it is part of your KRA or not?

Score ----------

Q6. Do you clearly understand your weaknesses & your strengths?

Score ----------

Q7. You feel confident all day long while you deliver any work, project, or assignment to the management?

Score ----------

Q8. You are reserved and do not know much about associates outside your team or workgroup?

Score ----------

Q9. You are interactive & have good communication skills?

Score ----------

Q10. You find yourself confident during meetings & discussions with clients, stakeholders & can handle conflicts smoothly & calmly.

Score ----------

It is good if you have scored 9 or 10 in all areas then you are ready to exceed expectations at your workplace & in your career roadmap and if you have scored less, we will soon be reversing the scores at the end of our journey of Change of Approach.

Chapter - 2

18 Success Principles for becoming an "Extraordinary" YOU

Success Principle 1

Find your "Happy Work"

Do you clearly understand your goal & the type of work that makes you happy? Do you know the purpose of the efforts you are putting daily when digging the same 9 meters down into the ground?

You cannot do & you must not do a work that does not make you happy! How can you spend 9 to 10 hours daily on something just to get a salary to pay a few bills? Wakeup! Out of the 24 hours, these 9-10 hours should be very precious for you that you spend at your workplace. Most of the people do not understand the fact that your overall career & financial growth depends upon how good you spend these first 9-10 hours of your day. Rest of the 15 hours are the after-effects, the experience, the result of what you accomplish in these first 9-10 hours of your day. The best accomplishment can be obtained only when you enjoy what you do, and even the challenges that come up related to this type of work make you feel alive.

You have just learnt the Rule of 24 meters down in 24 hours!

You can get these productive 24 hours only when you enjoy your work, and learning becomes your passion; when you regularly do research & analyse your own work daily for self-improvements.

Let us find out our Happy Work, to do this you need to use a notepad & pen, or you can simply write in mobile notes, laptop etc. but make sure you write it somewhere to ultimately find the work you really love.

You can read this book quickly just to look at what techniques & principles are best for you, but I highly recommend for all the readers that these exercises may require 5 to 10 mins but are the best mirror where you can clearly see yourself with your strengths & weaknesses.

So, do not skip this very important part of the book from where you will start preparing a base for yourself in this journey of success & growth.

- Activity: 1A -

You can write the answer in one or two words or in a sentence:

1) Hobbies - write any 3 favourite hobbies of yours (this can be what you love to do in free time)
2) Qualification, i.e. the learnt skill - specifically the degrees you own.
3) Certifications or workshops you attended since you are working as a professional.
4) Where do you spend most of your time - on social media or on YouTube, at the parties, with friends, family, games, learning new things online? Just analyse your past week to answer this.

5) If you spend time on YouTube - what kind of video you see (for example Spiritual, encouragement, learning related to your skills), or you see no videos at all.

6) On Social media and learning apps what kind of pages you have followed for an example: The fashion-related pages, skill-related, science, funny jokes, politics etc.

7) Write a couple of tasks that are part of your **existing Job Profile,** i.e., KRA's that you do at the office that makes you feel good & happy.

8) Other than assigned KRA, write what kind of work interests you the most. If given a chance, you would love to do this work which is not part of your existing KRA's.

9) You love teamwork or prefer to work individually and why?

10) You like to participate in employee engagement activities your organisation conducts on various occasions, or is it better to watch them from a distance or you do not like to be part of it at all.

11) How many breaks you like to take in between the work, be specific, for example, lunch break, tea breaks etc.

12) How many times did you deny any work or tasks given by your manager? Just for an example if your manager gave you 10 major tasks in the last one month then for how many tasks you said "No", or did not submit the task because maybe you did not like it, or you did not know how to do it?

Take a pause, keep the book aside for 5mins and write these answers as this is a very effective technique.

Let us understand the purpose of this exercise through the answers that Mr. ABC's shared with me. Hope you have written your answers, if not, then read Mr. ABC's answers to write yours later, you can do it anyway and make sure you pick the best answer based on the current working industry or profile of yours. This Mr. ABC is my friend and I did this exercise & interviewed him to actually analyse the result based on real-life examples.

Just to give a quick background, Mr. ABC's job was to dismantle the Generator engines at the start of his career and he never liked this work. He changed his job and joined a team where he is currently working as a "Designer" who prepares the design for water treatment plants. In simple words, when a mechanical engineer prepares some instructions & calculations related to the plant, the designer has to convert these pre-existing functionalities into a presentable layout. Mr. ABC somehow has a different area of interest other than the designing work he does, let's understand with the answers given by him during this interview:

Mr. ABC's answers:

Hobbies:

Answer 1. *Watching movies, photography, bike riding and going to the gym.*

Qualification:
Answer 2. *B.Tech after completion of 3 years diploma into Mechanical engineering.*

Certifications or learnt skills:
Answer 3. *Certification & training done on PDMS Software, AutoCAD software, MicroStation software.*

Spends his free time on:
Answer 4. *Mostly YouTube & love to attend parties and get together.*

Types of videos he likes to watch on YouTube:
Answer 5. *Funny videos, motivational video. Other than this, I like to watch new inventions & innovative videos related to latest technology-based water treatment plants; I want to strengthen my hands-on mechanical engineering.*

Social media pages that he follows:
Answer 6. *Politics, skill devolvement, science fiction related pages.*

The existing work that he likes:
Answer 7. *3D-modeling, preparing plant layouts and working as a trainer to help new associates develop their knowledge & skills, I also like to learn & practice new software & applications related to equipment design.*

Area of interest that are not part of the current job profile:
Answer 8. *If given a chance, I would like to develop my engineering skills, where I can independently calculate & develop the functionality of the water treatment plant. As per my existing job profile, I only prepare the designs & layouts based upon the pre-existing functionalities that are shared with me by a mechanical Engineer.*

A team player or an individual contributor:
Answer 9. *I prefer to work in a Team because it always provides scope & opportunity to get different points of views & ideas.*

Thoughts about Employee engagement activities & events that are conducted at the workplace:
Answer 10. *I enjoy participating in engagement activities & events that are conducted by the employee engagement team. It gives me time to recharge myself to perform better. I like to facilitate intra-departmental team building activities also.*

Working style & about the work breaks that are needed during the day:
Answer 10. *Total 3 breaks I take, short 15mins tea break while I reach office after checking my emails & planning my day's task then 1-hour lunch break and another short 15 to 30 minutes tea break in the evening.*

I cannot work continuously by sitting at one place for more than 2-3 hours. These short breaks help me stay active all day long.

If he said "No" to any ad-hoc task assigned to him:
Answer 11. *Yes, in the last month I did deny 2 tasks assigned to me and I know I could have completed those but was feeling a little bored with the same monotonous tasks as I already had a lot of layouts to prepare.*

Now based on these answers you, I or anybody who understands professional work & workplace atmosphere can analyse a couple of things here, i.e. Mr. ABC's working style, the type of work he likes to do and where he should be investing his time & energy for getting fast growth, and what kind of working culture he prefers.

When you do this exercise for yourself then logically & mystically both, you will be able to immediately analyse your current situation & none other than you who can best understand your own working style & the type of work you love to do!

We always wonder where to start from, be it preparing for an exam, be it starting a new venture, be it writing a book in my case! From where to start!!!

So, this exercise is the ANSWER to the question "WHERE to START", once you analyse yourself just like Mr. ABC did, you should be able to figure out what should be your first step.

Let us uncover the rest of the story here!

So Mr. ABC is a fun-loving person who loves partying with friends in his free time, his habit of going to gym & bike riding tells he is a fit sporty person. The pages he follows on social media categories shows that he has the ability to learn and grasp new things and innovation attracts him, which is a very good sign here.

Also, if we read the answers of Mr. ABC, he has done mechanical engineering & as per my discussion with him, his current work includes majorly the designing work based upon the pre-existing functionalities he receives from a mechanical engineer. He is good at his current work, but he gets attracted towards the process where he can involve himself into the initial stage, i.e., to work on the required calculations, research, analysis and the functionalities of the water treatment plants. He likes to go more in-depth to learn about the machine parts & its design. This is where he can explore more of his creative and innovative side.

He said he believes in teamwork, but when some ad hoc task was given to him within the team, his preference was not to do it, maybe he did not like the work, or he preferred to focus on his own work. As a team player, he surely likes to take feedback and suggestions for learning new creative ideas.

He is also very clear about his working style in which he prefers to take short breaks in between the work, and it is part of his work plan as it refreshes his mind to complete his task effectively, which again is a good sign to maintain work-life balance and mental peace.

Now when I gave this analysis to Mr. ABC, he did a quick introspection and the first step he took right after my discussion with him was:

- As you cannot completely shift your career path to a different direction in the middle of an unfinished journey, there are ways to add on to our existing skills to get to the TYPE of WORK we love the most! So, he is busy these days doing research on how to enhance his skills for working on machine functionalities; he is looking for certified courses and training to develop his skill set so that while continuing the existing work he gradually picks up the pace on the type of work he loves the most. This may take time like a year or so, but ultimately, he did get to realise after introspecting that this will be the work which would allow him to bring out his highest potential & maximum productivity at work.

You do not need to really understand what & how the water treatment plants function. This case study is to tell you how he was able to analyse his current situation & he now knows "FROM WHERE TO START". So, if I tell you in easy terms, Mr ABC is planning to gradually shift from "just the designing work stage" to the "pure mechanical engineering stage", where he can actually put creative ideas into functionalities based upon in-depth calculations & engineering work. Isn't it so amazing!

I really congratulate those who, just like me, do believe in the word "change". He showed his trust in me and changed his approach. His vision is clear now, he literally activated his ACTION MODE that I talked about earlier and I am sure the success will automatically follow his footsteps now!

- He now clearly knows that in order to find a new job for growth he needs to focus on a couple of things majorly - Role maturity, monetary benefits, and **the type of work** that will help him add value to his current areas of interest. Lastly, the most important for him is to look for **the culture of the company** as he is a jolly person, who loves to take breaks in between work, and enjoys participating in engagement activities and loves to work in a team. However, he needs to work on a couple of team-working skills, but surely these can be developed gradually with time. He cannot change his job just for getting a good salary grade & designation, as per his style of working he needs to work in a healthy happy working atmosphere to get to his maximum work productivity. So, **the culture of the company also matters to him;** he now knows what he wants & how he can get it.

It is not necessary that you need to always change the skill set to find the happy work that will be an incorrect approach. We first find Happy work & then we move towards skill development. This "HAPPY WORK" can be found from the existing profile or a new one. You must not flip your career upside down; you have to gradually upgrade yourself and shift yourself towards the area of interest. This should be a smooth & unhurried process where you grow yourself with this HAPPY WORK and find your highest potential without risking your current position.

So, like Mr. ABC you need to figure out a couple of things like what is your style of working, does the culture of the company really make an impact on your performance or can you avoid the culture and get motivated with a good salary package only! What are the skills that you need to add on to your current profile for remarkable productivity at work?

Think about it!

Success Principle 2

Our first alliance: "The Supervisor"

"Supervisor is a connecting bridge between associate & the management in any organisation, the only pivot that can easily congregate & disseminate the information to both side of this bridge."

- Shivali Tandon

We sometimes forget that to reach any destination we must keep moving and in order to do so, we may need to cross a river using a bridge to reach our destination. If we think that we can reach the destination without crossing this bridge, then we have to re-think again. The experience we gain while crossing this bridge helps us to build our own career roadmap. By now, you must have understood my meaning of this "bridge" is the **supervisor** or the **manager** at work. At all levels, other than the CEO, everybody has a supervisor depending upon the organisational hierarchy. As there are 2 sides of the coin, that means your bonding with your current supervisor can be good or bad. It is very important to check upon your relationship with your supervisor as **this has a major impact on your growth & career plans.** You cannot just take this relationship for granted. A good leader/supervisor of yours can really help you prepare your career growth plan by sharing with you your mistakes, weaknesses honestly and by providing the scope for improvements.

The first person who can encourage you, **who can motivate you or guide you correctly is your supervisor,** whether you believe it or not. It is ok if presently you do not feel this way. You may be having concerns with your present supervisor, he/she may not be supporting you up to your expectation, but now we will **change our approach** to eliminate this problem completely & forever.! Always remember that the change must first be brought upon by you before expecting the other person to change for you.

Get a clear expectation from your supervisor

Yes, I know if you do not like your manager/supervisor, you would never want to take any feedback from him. You do not want to trust him for that! Sometimes we feel we are way smarter than our supervisor & he/she is just sitting & enjoying the fruits of our efforts! Isn't it!

A manager or supervisor is someone who manages; he/she cannot sit with you & work all the time at the same pace. Yes, in new normal, a manager cum leader should sit with you & completely engage him/herself into the work assigned, but that is a Leadership skill which is to be understood by a Leader. The supervisors should understand that their assistance can be needed anytime by their team members who might get stuck at work. Failing to get this support and assistance from the supervisor, weakens this relationship.

We can't change them, but yes, we can do some amazing things to compel them to guide us correctly, to share the common vision for integrated career growth for each & every team member.

Now is it easy to compel someone to guide us? Not so easy, it demands time & energy to think about the other person and to give honest feedback.

Tell your supervisor very clearly that you need to have his feedback and assure him that you trust him on this. Ask him to share with you his clear expectation through assigned KRAs during feedback meetings.

Make sure to note down your area of expertise before the meeting, if you do not know how to find your "Happy Work" by now and did not actually try **activity: 1A** in the previous chapter then do it now to get a clear idea so that your KRA's can be aligned with the type of work that interest you the most and allows you to get maximum productivity at work, but be ready to expect a couple of non-interesting tasks as well to your KRA's and that's ok, be positive that you will learn something new out of it.

We do not have much of the flexibility to get all of our KRA's set as per our requirement as every organisation has its own way of working & requirements, so we need to find a middle way out that favours both the employer & the employee.

It is not at all easy for associates to "accept" the feedback, or to even talk about the weak points. You may not trust your supervisor initially, you may not like his way of working or even his behaviour, but only your supervisor can become the fuel for your engine. When did you last hear that a critic was humble while giving his opinions?

"Only courageous hearts can endure the bitterness of truth."

- Michael Bassey Johnson

So, we must change our approach towards what we "Expect" & what we "Accept". We must **welcome & cherish the most terrible feedback** we hear from someone senior in a hierarchy or even when your subordinates pinpoint your weaknesses. I know it is difficult to accept it, but it is important for our growth.

There are 2-3 types of people around us, a few who enjoy criticising us every now & then, they share their views about us not because they are concerned for us but because it does not really matter to them whether you win or lose, they do it out of habit or just for fun.

The other category we have is of the people who share their views about you, become a critic but with a genuine intention to see you grow. We need to just simply ignore who is who, what type of people you have around, and just focus on the issues or concerns they have raised. Not all concerns, feedback or criticism can be right but follow what your heart signals you. If you really feel the other person has a point, no need to respond to them with words, just start taking actions to change it completely, whatever it takes - hard work, time, or any new skill addition.

Whatever I have achieved so far in my life is firstly because I have a firm belief in God and the second **major credit I give to those who always bullied me, told me that I could never win,** those who always have shared the harshest comments. Initially, it did hurt me a lot, but **they are the reason I responded back, not with my tongue, but silently with my ACTIONS,** these actions do not include any revenge, *Nah, not at all!* Action for me is to keep working harder, to achieve the impossible.

On the other side, I have immense respect for those who have given their honest feedback as they really wanted me to grow in my life. **Trust me; this is the essence of success for so many people.** The more difficult hurdles you find in your path, the higher you jump to cross them.

From now on, from this very moment you must change your approach, those who annoy you, hate you, think you are worthless, do not waste your time responding back to them with your words or anger, or by thinking more about these people. **In fact, respond to them with your actions, be more focussed, be ready to accept the feedback, make the changes** *& tadaah!!* We are so many steps ahead from them, so close to our actual goal of life, so close to the success we deserve. **Your manager will surely start sharing his feedback with you when he finds you in high spirit and if he can sense your learning attitude.**

Take these criticisms and honest feedback from a good manager very positively. Also, ask your manager to help you understand the parameters based on which your performance will be monitored, there is no point of asking it at the time of the review meeting. Clarity should be taken from your manager well in advance at the time your KRA's are getting finalised.

Never forget that **even the most terrible person can teach you an excellent lesson in life.**

We should thank those around us who become our critics from time to time; they are the triggers that ignite our life engine for CHANGE. What matters is the way we respond back to these people. Respond wisely only through your actions. If they say you lack these skills, then it is great, you will learn some new skills because of them. If they say, you cannot manage your work properly then start making proper work "to do" list, keep track of the work and submit the work at the given timeline. If they say you don't have good communication skills, then find ways to improve your communication each day, interact more, get online training in those 15 hours you get after signing off from the office. You will end up thanking these people after so many years because you were able to achieve greater heights by acting upon their criticism or genuine feedback for your own good. You just have to change the way you think with a more positive approach.

Do not be hesitant

So we are now ready to accept the best and also the worst feedback from people around us, and we are determined not to respond to the most terrible comments we hear about us at the workplace. This does not mean to just give up & accept if we are guilty, but it actually means that we will let our action speak for us, these actions will itself do the rest of the work.

The next approach is to check upon how "hesitant" we are to ask questions, how hesitant we are to share our viewpoint, how hesitant we are to interact openly with our manager. A person who keeps on **putting their thoughts on the table will always succeed.** You must keep sharing your suggestions while it is wrong to expect that each and every one of your ideas will be acted upon. There is no harm in sharing your thoughts & ideas if it does not have even 10% of the impact on the final decision. Be it the development of the building, be it the new application your company is going to launch, be it any new product launch, be it new sales or marketing techniques, do not hesitate to share your thoughts with your supervisor.

First, it will help you learn more about the topic and the

trend as you will have to do a little research before sharing your ideas with someone. So many times, I have noticed that people who have so many great ideas are hesitant and have fear while sharing those. For example, *"what if I share my idea with my supervisor and he himself will take credit for it"*. However, so many companies nowadays have open-door policies, conducting regular town halls as the Senior management is easily available to listen to such problems & feedback. But this is not possible every time to go to the Sr. management to share your concerns, that is why I mentioned at the beginning that the SUPERVISOR for me is the connecting bridge we have to cross at any cost! You must do what is right; no one can snatch the knowledge you have.

It is important to trust your manager, to have this kind of bond with your manager that he always is happy to listen to your idea. If he likes the idea and is generous, then he never will miss to reward you. No matter if a supervisor is trying to grab the benefits alone, be assured that sooner or later, the management discovers the truth.

> *"Ideas can be stolen but not the mind from where that idea originated, the implementation of that idea will anyhow require the creator of it."*
>
> \- Shivali Tandon

In fact, the best part between a manager & its team relationship is that if the manager starts to trust its team member, the team member always has the free hand to share ideas & get the relevant rewards. So, start building this bond. Let your manager also understand your worth. As you never expressed yourself, shared your ideas & suggestions, never had tried to do extra research on the current assignments, then how will the manager be able to understand your worth? *"jo dikhta hai wo bikta hai" i.e.,* it is well said by someone that until or unless you do not show your work, it will not sell.

To recall quickly what we have just learnt to have a whole new approach to:

- get clear expectations from our managers no matter how worse the face-off will be, but we must accept it, do it in your next discussion meeting & of course when you are ready to bring about the "change".
- Secondly, we will no longer hesitate to share our ideas with management & with the manager in specific, be ready to take extra initiatives by doing some research about the topic.

Time to relax when your Manager is not around??

Aha! You heard it right... awesome feeling when the manager is on long leave or travelling due to work. No one is there to monitor your work, to pinpoint you, to question you!

The biggest mistake many associates do is that they become complacent, actionless & inactive for a while in the absence of their manager. This becomes an *aha!* moment for most of us.

Please try to understand that you are working for the organisation, not only for someone who is a team leader, manager or supervisor of yours. I know it is a basic human tendency to act carelessly and with less zeal, to respond slowly when no one is monitoring us.

In personal life also, had it not been our parents to check upon our sleeping habits, we would have never been able to attend our school or college lectures on time. Even if not the parents, someone in the family or a friend was always there to help us inculcate and adapt the best practices. To build those habits that are needed for healthy better living. So this is the same attitude, we may be working hard enough & then suddenly one day we take a break from work, become inactive because our manager is not present, or he is busy with some other work, there can be any reason for it.

Everybody needs someone to guide, to suggest, to monitor us, that is why we have a set hierarchy at the organisation. Yes, there are a couple more reasons to have a hierarchy at the organisation, but in simple words, the CEO alone cannot monitor each & every single activity that's happening within the organisation and with each associate. However, the CEO always gets to know reality sooner or later!

Sometimes our manager puts a lot of pressure on our shoulders; sometimes we want to take a break from work! Like most of you, for me as well, that was the best time to relax a little when the manager was on leave or away from the office even for a couple of hours or a day! But **gradually, I had to change my approach!** The same old approach to become inactive never helped me out to learn something new; actually, I realised that it could become a huge hindrance in my growth.

I heard this in one of the workshops on developing leadership skills that *"a true manager is the one who has such a strong team which can work well in his/her absence & deliver the desired work on time."* It is hard to digest, but such leaders can foster amazing teams that can deliver any task even in his own absence. This can be done by a leader who is not at all insecure about his own job & is able to foster future leaders at the organisation. I truly respect such leaders.

As an associate, we somehow love the **inactive state** when it is needed the most. Apart from it, as I mentioned above that you are not working for any team leader or manager, **you are working towards a shared goal of the organisation that will benefit you & the employer both.** So, when the manager is not around, **it is your responsibility to work more sincerely & cautiously!** Obviously, it does not mean you try to overshadow your manager, not at all!

We somehow feel that when the manager is not around, no one can notice us, but except your manager, everybody else keeps an eye upon you to see how you perform & present your work in your supervisor's absence. At least when your supervisor is there with you, you are answerable only to one person, but in his absence, you are answerable to many, in higher hierarchies or skip levels.

"How many tea-breaks & chill-out breaks have you taken?"

It is very common that when your supervisor is not in the office & team members genuinely feel less burdened; they love to take breaks from work every now & then. People around you may have this pre-existing notion in mind that *"Ahhh!! Can you see, the team is chilling out & has no work, as the manager is on leave".*

Do not get me wrong here; let's not become a person who would like to react to such childish comments, also let's not avoid our usual daily tea breaks at work. **Work-life balance is a very important element of your employment and we must maintain it.** I would love to work with the same pace in the absence of my manager because firstly I am working for the organisation and not for the manager alone. Secondly, **I am working each day sincerely to see my own progress.** Skipping the tasks for a day or so & then suddenly feeling pressurised because the work deadline is near & manager has also joined back, this will surely result in poor performance and will reduce my work efficiency!

While I was busy enjoying my "inactive" mode in the manager's absence, the time did not stop, the tasks & assignments were not stopping from adding up to my "to do" list.

Third and the most important point, we can fool everyone, but we can never fool ourselves. It feels good to enjoy this inactive state for a day or so, but ultimately no one is getting affected by this, not even your manager, not even your organisation in the long-term, but only "you" will be affected with this.

Let us give our brain some exercise to do so that you can relate to the problem & deeply inculcate the solution here.

Scenario 1:

Think for a while that in the absence of the manager, the 2nd-level manager (your boss's boss) the manager's manager approaches you to provide data that is urgently required, but you were not on your desk, or you are working from a remote location and you were offline or away from the system when your manager's manager is looking for you. You missed to respond & obviously your manager has no idea about it! Who is going to be responsible for the delay as the requirement was extremely critical? Maybe your leader will have to face the consequences & so does the team.

Scenario 2:

Contradictory to this if you would have responded on time, even if you did not know how to complete that task, surely you have informed the manager's manager with the required status of this work. **Not every task can be completed in your manager's absence as their guidance & suggestion have a major impact on the deliverables.** That is why they are the managers & we are working under their supervision, but out of 100 times, you should be happy if you were able to deliver the work even 20 times correctly to the manager's manager or some other stakeholders.

Even if we did not perform well, we had learnt something out of it. The manager's manager is also aware of your efforts now on the given task.

Now you have to decide what is your approach! You want to act as per the first scenario or as per the second one.

Let go of the burden & work pressure that your manager has transferred upon your shoulder!

I wish every associate could get a manager they had imagined in their dreams. Imagine having a caring, lovable & cool leader but knock-knock! We are talking about leaders who can foster us and not about friends who can support us. One does not have all 5 fingers of equal length. It is not about the leaders or someone's traits, but no one has all 100 traits incorporated into their life system, which are liked by all.

Everybody is different, your manager may have 99 good things that you like about him & may have 1 thing which you may not like. We cannot assemble our managers or leaders as per our personalised needs. You are feeling too burdened to handle the pressure showered upon you by your current manager & the manager may not even realise it.

It is better to focus on how to change the overall situation instead of putting efforts in changing your manager, as all your efforts will be useless. Also, why do we want anybody to change for us? We should be capable enough to find the best out of every negative situation; we should be capable of working under any manager anytime.

If you are expecting that your manager or mentor will go easy on you for work deliverables, then it can happen only in imaginations. Another stakeholder higher in the hierarchy is expecting the same from your manager (the manager's manager) & this stakeholder may have built pressure already on your manager's shoulders.

Actions speak louder than words, so try to take as many actions as you can to strengthen your position at work. You must speak when it is needed the most, don't fight for it, i.e. we just learnt not to be hesitant & that principle applies here too.

Discuss with your manager that you are unable to showcase

your highest potential because of the way the tasks have been assigned by him/her. Out of the 10 concerns, if your manager can address even 5 concerns, then also it is a big improvement in the current situation.

Maybe your manager may suggest some better ways to handle the pressure. Sometimes because of critical deliverables, you need to go beyond your comfort levels, but again a balance should be maintained.

"Work is a very important element of your life,
but it cannot become your LIFE alone."

- Shivali Tandon

There are ways to act calmly under pressure; it is normal to get annoyed if your manager checks with you after every 30mins for the status of your work. So, it's time to analyse your working responsibilities and to create a perfect planner for yourself so that we get rid of the pressure building situation at the workplace. This type of planning can be implemented at your home as well.

Proactive Approach: 2A

No Stress, High-performance voyage

You call it a PLAN, but I define it like so:

P - Prepare | L - Learn | A - Apply | N - Navigate

When you are feeling too much of work pressure, please make sure to take these actions immediately, which include a Proactive approach:

1. PREPARE - Prepare the list of activities/tasks that you have on your plate.

The Proactive approach: Start preparing a simple point to point "To-do List" daily. This is one best habit you can start developing to see wonderful results.

2. LEARN - A task becomes easy if you have knowledge about it, i.e., to have a clear background about the task that has been assigned to you.

The Proactive approach: Only your **skillset & knowledge can save your time.** If you feel you are getting a task related to the work you are not well versed about, then **Learn** it until you get it right. This will gradually reduce the ETA (a term used to measure the expected time of completion of any work) for completing a task. Prioritise your work when you have too much of work added on to the "To do" or "task list".

Priorities can vary from person to person so either pick up the easiest yet highest priority task that can be completed easily to let go off the work pressure or pick up the most critical & important task first. In case there is any critical task that is half done & needs a little more research, then take a small break from that particular task and try to pick small chunks of other tasks that require minimum attention and are part of your daily work routine. This is how you can keep yourself motivated by completing or striking out these small chunks of tasks from the "To-do list".

3. APPLY - Time to convert your work plan into Actions

The Proactive approach: To know the priority you will have to check the dates on which these tasks have been assigned to you, which means you are now able to track the number of days/hours you have spent completing one task or the other. This third phase is the implementation of **"apply the strategy"** phase, where you start working on the highest priority task.

Just for an example:

Category of Tasks	**Assigned on this date**	**Priority of the task**	**Progress & status**
Task A	Date	Medium	Yet to start
Task B	Date	Low	Yet to start
Task C	Date	Critical	In progress
Task D	Date	High	Done

The "To Do" or "tasks" list is not restricted to this format only, you can draft your own "To Do" or "tasks list" as per your convenience but **keep it short & realistic** so that it turns out to be an effective work management technique. Do not spend too much time to design or fill this task list; the purpose is to save time not to waste it!

4. <u>**NAVIGATE**</u> - It is Time to navigate the ship to finish the voyage.

The Proactive approach: When we plan correctly, then we always pick the right priority and can apply the correct approach to complete the task. Now we are into the navigation stage and are ready to sail the ship in the direction we wanted it to move.

Do not keep the task with you after its completion or wait for the manager to show up with another reminder for it. As soon as you **ensure the quality of the work, do a last final review,** and **share it** with your manager. Navigation is actually stress releasing phase for me, as soon as the task is submitted to the concerned party the less burdened I feel. Pick up another task, navigate then pick up the third task, navigate and so on.

Do not get easily distracted with any additional task that keeps on adding to your list; your focus should be very clear about the "priority" you set earlier.

The result after the successful implementation:

PREPARED -> LEARNT -> APPLIED -> NAVIGATED
= No Stress, High performance voyage

Always remember no matter how many tasks you get in a day with deadlines, it is important to plan & navigate it correctly as per the decided timelines. Unplanned activities & work approach will always result in pressure building. We will never be able to get rid of the work, as we did not plan it correctly & with time the tasks keep on getting piled up one after the other.

Success Principle 3

"The AB Principle"

Whether you believe it or not, but this AB principle has a major impact on your work performance & career growth. Let us understand this in the upcoming sections, but before I share any further details about it, I would love to engage you in a small brain activity again.

You do not need any pen or paper to do this. I have a couple of scenarios for you, just fit yourself into the scenario & **notice your first response.** You must be completely honest with yourself, like 100% honest as no one is going to ask what & how you reacted under the given situation but yes just think of the first & the foremost response that comes to your mind.

For example - While Shivali was walking, she suddenly saw a pit on the ground, what response do you expect from her?

"I would have changed my lane" or,

"I would have jumped over the pit", or

"I would have fallen into the pit as I was busy checking my mobile phone".

That is it! You just have to imagine your first response on the given scenarios that are mentioned below. Moreover, it will be a fun exercise!

Scenario:

You are part of a new project where a manager & a lead are there to plan the working of the project. Other than the Managers, the team involves 3 team members who will be practically working on the project from scratch. This project requires a variety of skills & knowledge that all three team members possess. The task will be the same for all three members & so the performance parameters remain the same for all.

The project managers have all the details about your skills & knowledge, but they are not sure how the team members will pick a particular task as the project is completely new & it requires efforts from each of the team members. Now imagine that you are one of the team members out of these three, sitting in a conference room with 2 leaders & 2 other team members with you.

Managers share the targets & plans for execution and present the list of tasks. So according to basic mathematics, all 3 individuals should receive an equal proportion of tasks by the managers.

The 2nd Team member had performed average in his last assignment, so the managers are aware of his speed at work, having the same skill but as his working style is different, he needs more time to complete day to day tasks.

The 3rd team member is so fast in his work that he completes the tasks before time as he wants to feel relaxed during evening tea break & he tries to complete the task so fast that sometimes he makes mistakes as well, i.e., the quality of the work is compromised.

Now, imagine yourself as the 1st team member here who is waiting for the task to get assigned thinking about how the work will be divided among 3 team members.

Managers have assigned the maximum number of tasks to you, or you can say a major part of the project has been assigned to you & the rest of the work was distributed among the other 2 members.

I request you to re-read the above scenario once again so that you are picking up the best honest response here, as this will really help you to understand the AB principle in-depth and accordingly will have its impact on your performance from now on.

When you receive the maximum tasks, it would surely be a time taking endeavour, may be tough as well and would require more brainstorming. So, what was the first thought that came to your mind.

No one is going to ask about how you reacted to this scenario. Stay true to yourself as it is important to understand yourself first.

Choose any one of the responses (thought) honestly!!

First Thought - This is so unfair, when tasks require the same skill set then it should be distributed in equal proportion, do you agree or disagree? Think about the response in your mind.

Second Thought - As I have been assigned the maximum work, I need to spend more time & will have to put extra efforts, I will talk to my manager to reduce my task & to give it to other members in equal proportion. Is this the right step to take or not? Think about this in your mind.

Third Thought - Great! My manager surely finds me capable of handling these many tasks and that is why he has chosen me for the same. I will try my level best to complete it on time with accuracy.

Write the thought no. that you have chosen
above out of the 3 options...

____________________??

Now keep in mind the very first response that came to your mind out of these three thoughts; obviously, all three thoughts are opposite to each other under the same scenario, so it is not possible for you to have all three thoughts as your answer/response. Pick any 1 considering your current organisation culture and your current job description. No one is going to judge you here at all. At least not me!

Every feeling & thought will sooner or later be expressed in our behaviour, so let us find out what will be the "REACTION", or you can say "EXPRESSION" to the above-mentioned responses!

Corresponding the above thoughts, my reaction will be expressed or can be sensed in a specific way or manner.

With thought no. 1 - I will creep while I work. Something will keep bothering me as if I am left with no option but to sit at the system, spending hours & hours to complete the tasks because I have received a huge part of it. I have been feeling so burdened since the beginning that I am unable to concentrate on my work properly. Also, I see the other 2 members working so calmly as they do not have this much work! My mind wants to perform well but somehow feels that injustice has been done to me.

Since these thoughts linger in my mind, I would never be able to find my maximum work potential.

With thought no. 2 - I am so carefree & not able to accept the decision of assigning a major part of the work to me. I am planning to talk to the manager to convey to him my disinterest about the extra tasks. Also, this is clearly visible to my manager that I am not at all happy with the way tasks have been distributed in the team. Even if there is no option to change this decision, my mind is reacting in a revolting manner that I will not take a lot of stress, and I would complete the said tasks as per my mood & convenience. I have been assigned most of the tasks as compared to the other two members, then why should I take a lot of pressure even if the other two members have completed half of their work. There is no comparison, why should I care about it!

With thought no. 3 - I am so happy that among the whole team, **my manager can clearly notice my work potential.** It is so amazing that the manager had trusted me with such major task of this project, and this means the work dependency is more upon me, i.e. I am being valued. I know this demands a lot of extra work, research & efforts to complete the additional task here but at least I am ready to put my 100% effort to get it done **timely & accurately. My mind is not at all stressed but focussed because my mind has accepted it as a new challenge at work.** If I can manage the time & work properly, I will be able to complete the task accurately, no matter how much work proportion has been assigned to me.

These positive vibes coming out of your body & mind as a reaction will surely keep you motivated throughout. I hope you can now understand the correct approach by yourself now! With only one scenario, we can notice **three different reactions.**

Now to analyse a little more about your AB quotient, let's understand the above scenario by knowing more about Attitude & Behaviour Principle, i.e., "The AB principle".

Attitude involves the mind's tendency to certain values, people & ideas as we just found in the above scenario. The above thought that came to my mind is my tendency to look at the situation, the tendency to consider it either as a challenge, as a new opportunity, as a learning or as stress, as a hindrance in my growth, or as an unfair decision that was forcefully imposed upon me. These tendencies build our ATTITUDE! This attitude towards various situations result in a specific kind of "Reaction" that becomes our next quotient, i.e. "Behaviour" and what is behaviour?

Behaviour involves our actual **reaction** towards something, expression of feelings through our body language.

In simple words "What we feel" & "How we react" throughout the day is our AB quotient.

The balance between both attitude & behaviour is so important at work. Slightest disturbance in any one of the quotients will reduce your work potential, which is responsible for your overall Career growth & success in life! However, attitude & behaviour can be explained through many definitions here, but in simple terms, we have 2 types: "positive" attitude & behaviour towards various scenarios or "negative" attitude & behaviour towards various scenarios.

This above scenario is just one example to understand the principle of attitude & behaviour in one's life. This AB principle is not restricted to this scenario or situation but can be applied to our day-to-day responses & reactions. **The more positive your AB quotient is, the better is your potential in life.**

To see the best version of yourself during any situation, start analysing your AB quotient. You will be amazed by the results. **By having a correct AB quotient in your life, you can achieve anything anytime, anywhere!**

I had personally experienced the magic of Attitude & Behaviour in every single area of my life, be it the workplace, family, relationships, tough times, face-off with challenges etc. I was able to encounter many victories in life by **considering every problem as an opportunity to learn something new, by considering every failure of my life as an opportunity to find out the best version of me.** Becoming an author this year is one live example of it. I am writing this book by taking out time from my busy schedule, while working as a professional like you all, by going beyond every limitation I have in front of me. I am doing all this only by maintaining a positive AB quotient in my life.

One can test their own AB quotient only when he or she encounters a real-life problem or a scenario. That is the best time to check upon our attitude & behaviour quotient. The scenario that led me to become an author is COVID-19, the year of fear! Yes, I tested positive with the critical condition of my health. Those 21 days of isolation could have been depressing and torturing, but because I try to keep my AB quotient strong in every situation, this has helped me **bring out something from nothing.** I have loved writing since I was a child and during those 21 days of separation from the outer world, I decided to work hard toward my passion and a lifelong dream to become an author! This would not have been possible without having a positive AB quotient.

I had utilised those 21 days for understanding my passion as I was on a long sick leave and was unable to leave the bed because of the weakness due to the COVID-19 infection in my lungs. I always tell my friends, had it not been these 21 days of isolation, I would have never witnessed the highest potential in me. But surely this is not the end, the highest potential is no set destination, where once you reach you can sit ideally & do nothing. It is a process, a never-ending process, the more we polish our life with a positive AB quotient, the more closer we get to reach our highest potential.

From today make sure you "change your approach" toward the problems & issues you face daily. The person who had the "3rd thought" had considered it as an opportunity to learn more & to explore his/her highest potential at work by keeping a positive attitude or behaviour which undoubtedly would reflect in their ACTIONS. That is what we all need to inculcate in our attitude & behaviour while encountering the worst of the situations at the workplace.

The quantity does not matter when you have a quality product which is prepared with a lot of effort & with your highest potential. So, from today, from now, take every single task as an opportunity to polish your skills! It is time to change your approach **from Why me to Try me!** I am not asking you to take unnecessary work or to be an opportunist to snatch other people's work; this again reflects a negative attitude. Feel satisfied with whatever work is assigned to you & at the same time be prepared mentally and physically to put all your efforts to complete any new assignments without considering it as a burden.

Always remember that your work does not make you special, rather YOU make the work special. This can only happen when you have a stable, strong & positive attitude towards your job.

Let us understand the key to stimulate our "highest potential" by maintaining an outstanding AB quotient at our workplace; I call it the **AB model.**

Attitude-Behaviour Model: 3A

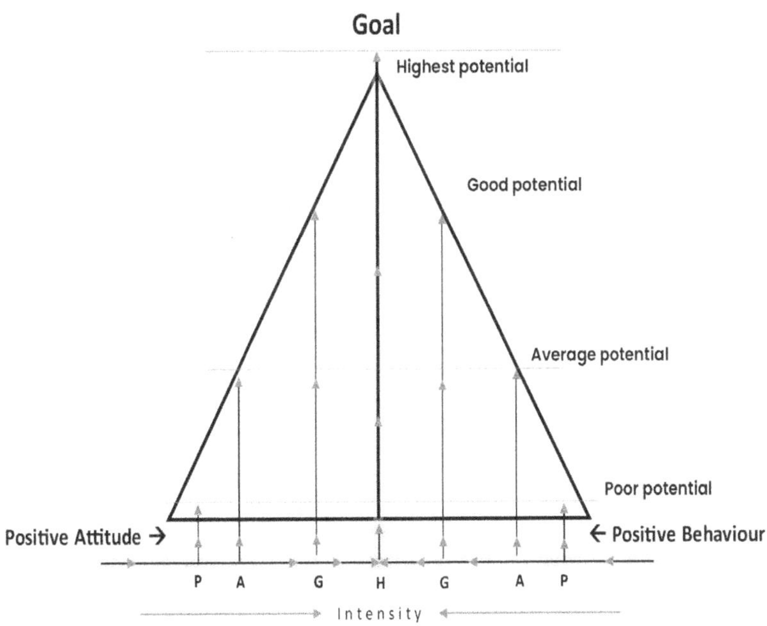

The more intense our **Positive Attitude,** the more constructively our **positive behaviour** develops, which ultimately results in high-performance potential. Points "P", "A", "G" are respectively depicting the ***intensity* of our positive AB quotient,** i.e., by reflecting Poor, Average & Good Potential. Point "H" depicts the highest potential which can be attained by having a very strong positive AB quotient.

The Highest potential point is the "GOAL" which indeed is the best version of ours, that is the **Destination** where we have to reach.

Increase the intensity of looking at things positively with a balanced AB quotient. The weaker your AB quotient, the lower is the potential at the workplace.

Have a look at the **AB model 3A** & find yourself, where your AB quotient lies, a change of approach towards any upcoming situation or problem can instantly change our position in the graph. Let us all choose to keep moving upwards from the lowest potential to the peak point where we encounter our highest potential at work or in our personal life.

Other than having a strong AB quotient, there are a couple of other factors that impact our overall AB quotient in general:

• Jealousy & healthy competition

Do not confuse healthy competition with "jealousy". Competition is a good sign of growth, but that should be a healthy competition. It should not bypass basic work ethics. It should not be reflected in your behaviour as a jealousy factor towards your peers, subordinates & co-workers. As soon as any team member has this feeling of jealousy, it can literally affect the team bonding, no matter how strong it was earlier. To avoid this just focus on your efforts & keep checking upon your AB quotient each day. There should be no place for jealousy.

• Gratitude is the Key

There is this beautiful process of saying "thank you" which is to simply show gratitude towards other associates who help you, assist you, and support you. Never forget to say thanks!

You may not see this, but it has an invisible power to strengthen your bond with every single person you show your gratitude towards. The other person will never forget you obliged him with deep gratitude for the work they did for you. You can say "thank you" to anybody even to the Junior staff member at your office, the housekeeping boy who cleans the floor for you daily. A thank you said beautifully can make that person happy; this is how nobody will ever stop helping each other at the workplace. This adds value to a healthy work culture.

• Stop bragging or saying this to others "I am the SENIOR; you are the JUNIOR!"

This is the worst approach one can have & you will not even realise that due to this **your positive attitude will someday become your "Attitude problem"** as you would always focus on drawing a line with the attitude of being a SENIOR in your team & would make others realise again & again that he/she is a JUNIOR team member.

If because of your Senior grade or designation you never thought that your subordinates are eligible to provide suggestions or are not capable enough to get involved in certain decisions and you keep on hiding new updates from them, then you have a very negative AB quotient. In such cases, you are damaging the performance of the team as well as limiting your own growth. Never forget that the organisational policies, guidelines are applicable to each employee and the performance evaluation is to be done for all, i.e. all employees are considered equal irrespective of their profile & designations. The reason why hierarchies are set in any organisation is just that **the higher we go in the hierarchy, the more responsible we become.** If you really want to grow & want to become a successful leader in future, then do not let yourself get caught up in this notion of "Senior & Junior".

Developing Soft skills through "Correct Attitude & Behaviour"

Now when we can strengthen our positive AB quotient, it is time to express it through soft skills.

Do not consider building Soft skills like qualification or a specific degree you would master upon because there will be no benefit in just mastering 1-2 soft skills to win the battle.

Soft skill is like a pool that has a combination of skills, starting from people skills, social skills, your character & personality traits, communication skills, attitudes, career attributes, your social & emotional intelligence.

These Soft Skills really help all of us to work well with others, to perform well in any area of life and for achieving our life goals & career goals together. In the initial years of my own career, I never tried to think this deeply about the need for Soft skills. I thought that a warm smile, respectful gestures, our manners, and decency are enough to get us going.

But gradually I realised the exact opposite of this, which is that the stronger your soft skills are the better the scope for growth in life.

You believe it or not, but *"everything starts & ends only in the most complicated circuit ever to exist, i.e. "our Brain". The way our brain thinks & responds has a major impact on what type of life we will be having.*

\- Shivali Tandon

If you have heard about the Power of Positive "thinking", the Power of subconscious "Mind", our life is the result of our "thoughts", all these statements have one common connecting hub which is "THE BRAIN".

As I just mentioned above, we don't have to learn soft skills like a theory, but **soft skills are to be developed with time which is completely based on practical experiences.**

What I have learned in the last couple of years is that soft skills are not at all like a syllabus from a B.Tech course where you master one topic, score good and hold the degree in hand. After you get the job you do not write that theory, you make your own code based upon the language you had mastered during B.Tech.

Pre-existing technical codes were never there, and one developer was there to write that **first code** to make one application working. This is just an example to understand about Soft Skills very clearly. Theoretical knowledge is available everywhere on the internet, but actual learning starts only when you apply the theory. For rooting these soft skills into the core of our mind, we really need to practice them on every occasion, just like we perform our daily routines. Build such good soft skills that they become your habit and not just stay as a theory in your mind. Convert this theory into thoughts & apply during the best possible moments.

Type of Soft skills that strengthen Positive Attitude & Behaviour

You will easily find the existence of "Attitude" & "Behaviour" in every single soft skill which is mentioned below. You must focus on the change of approach towards each skill to build a positive attitude & behaviour within you. Soft skill is a huge topic for discussion, and here we are going to understand the basics & its applicability.

People Skill

Patterns of behaviour and interactions with people.

I really liked the way the Portland Business Journal has described the people skills as:

- Ability to effectively communicate, understand, and empathise.
- Ability to interact with others respectfully and develop productive working relationships to minimise conflict and maximise rapport.
- Ability to build sincerity and trust; moderate behaviours (less impulsive) and enhance agreeableness.

Reference: Rifkin, H. "Invest in people skills to boost bottom line" Retrieved on 2009-10-14.

Our change of approach will come into action now when we are able to communicate with people effectively by understanding their problems & concerns, and at the same time by empathising instead of sympathising. To respect the other person, you need to create a bond or a relationship with that person. You cannot respect someone genuinely from your heart without knowing that person, without bonding with that person as a manager, supervisor, or a subordinate. Try to build people skills by changing your thought process towards the other person.

I do not want you to learn the definitions to conduct real-time actions, but instead, I would be happy to see you taking actions from this very moment. **Let us stop being judgmental from now about anyone we meet at the office or in personal life, let us stop making fun of the work he/she does, let us stop focusing on the work the other person does, let's respect everyone around us, let's apply wisdom to understand them, let's provide them with a little space.**

Trust me, if you are thinking that this people's skill is all about giving & giving then you are mistaken here, as whatever we are doing is for our own good. Those who have maintained good relationships at the workplace with everyone by reflecting strong positive people's skills are the most successful. Healthy competition is great, but this should not stop you from helping someone at work, being the senior in the team is great but learning something new from your peers & subordinates is a sign of showing respect to what others know better than you.

I told you already, everything you read in this book requires the "change of approach," i.e. the change in the thought process. It is not a yoga exercise that needs to be practised daily. From the moment you command your mind to develop these skills, then boom! You are all set to reflect the same in your actions. **The only thing you need is the POWER to CHANGE your thought process.**

Social Skills

I truly believe that to have strong social skills; you should have the essence of "people skills" as well. That is the base of every conversation we do socially. Strong social skills can save from nervousness & embarrassment while you interact. At an organisational level, the social skills include empathy, team coordination, cooperation, verbal & written communication, i.e. how you convey your message clearly via emails or in chats, your message should always reflect a polite tone. And next in the list is non-verbal communication that involves your body language, your attention during the meeting, eye contact, your facial expressions.

Listening to others carefully & to address their concerns timely and correctly are also part of social skill for building healthy relationships within your team or outside of your team at the workplace. Being persuasive is another social skill, at times you may find your team member not performing well or distracted, or he may not be able to understand the complexity of work, in such cases this skill can really help you build a strong, healthy relationship. It requires a lot of effort, correct information & proper reasoning to change another person's attitude & behaviour towards something, be it a small task or the implementation of a new business model or introducing a new process into the system. You should be reasonable while conveying your decision as well as be empathic while listening to their point.

At the workplace, what I have learnt in the last many years is that **you never work alone, you cannot work alone**, it's always a collective action due to which the result comes out to be either Good or Bad. Directly or indirectly our work which we really think is an "individual task" is impacted by this social world and with our surroundings. If we only think about this "individual", then who is going to work for the shared goal and vision that organisation has, as for them it is always a collaborative effort from start to end. Of course, at the social level, we are representing our organisation as an "individual", but when hundreds & thousands of such individuals together work under one brand name, they become "one" with a shared goal & vision.

Communication Skill

From the above, we now understand that we need to be a good listener, we need to empathise while we interact with others, but there is also one other important aspect of communication. How we communicate is the one skill, which cannot be overlooked, as it is all about the effective interaction we do at our workplace and outside the workplace.

We should use correct mediums to convey our message, become a good listener, use correct language & tone to convey our message to have clear, smooth interactions within the team, and with stakeholders or clients. Imagine every single person around you interacting with each other only through sign languages, without words & voice, somehow the message will have the same impact, but the voice has multiple expressions, i.e.

through our tone, the words we choose while we speak, the aura we carry while we interact with each other, surely the "voice" has its own impact on others.

Have a habit of smiling decently while you share the most critical information with someone, while you give the most critical feedback to someone, or while listening to them in return. This smile automatically softens our tone while we interact. If we listen to neuro experts, it is found that certain hormones are released when we smile, serotonin one amongst those balances our feelings of well-being and happiness and helps us remain calm & stress-free. So, a decent smile, while we interact, does not harm at all; it will make the communication effective. However, you cannot console people for any mishappening that had happened with them by having the same smiling gesture. Use your wisdom to know when & how this smiling expression must be used as you need to be very sensitive depending upon the situations you are dealing with.

Social & Emotional Intelligence

Social & emotional intelligence helps us build strong bonds professionally; this bond of trust if developed correctly, can be the reason for unlimited success based on the AB model. The social & emotional intelligence quotient carries the extract of above three main skills we had just learnt about, the people skill, soft skill & communication skill. Let us refresh what we have learnt above quickly and inculcate these skills from now onwards:

Proactive Approach: 3B

1. Effective listening.
2. Having good conversation skills.
3. Listening to other people's ideas with an open-minded approach.
4. By building a decent reputation at your workplace.
5. By becoming a good observant.
6. By paying attention to what is happening around.
7. Showing trust & confidence in your peers, subordinates, and your friends.
8. Building a positive persuasive approach towards others.
9. By deleting the word "sympathy" from your dictionary & focusing clearly on "empathy".
10. Create a positive aura in your surrounding by fostering the positive AB quotient into day-to-day activities you do.
11. Introspect every time when other people share their concerns.
12. Accept the most critical feedback to find a better version of "self".
13. **Start responding instead of "reacting" to any conflict or situation.**

All the above skills need to be re-read & applied from now on in any given situation. If you really want to inculcate these skills permanently, then practice them daily as & when applicable. I would suggest you click a photograph/screenshot of these 13 requirements from your mobile phone for easy access. Try to read these 13 points daily for the next 21 days to merge them into your daily responses.

Success Principle 4

Why does your company not need you anymore?

Before we go further, please note that this principle & the next one is amongst the most important 'changes of approach' you will need to quickly align yourself with success in the new normal.

Also, I want you to remind yourself about **activating your ACTION MODE** as among all the other principles this specific approach will require maximum implementation.

Now quickly think about any 2-3 reasons the company does not want you anymore or maybe can ask you or any associate to leave the organisation at any moment?? Why? Base your thought considering the impact of the decision, is it because of you? Or because of the organisation or because of any other reason that comes to your mind... Think Think!!

Align your goal with the vision of the company to see yourself grow fast

If you work at an organisation and spend 8 to 9 hours of your day at the office completing the tasks one after the other, that means you have been hired for something that adds value to the company's vision.

Years have been passed, but you have this feeling like nothing has changed for you! You are at the same job level, were at the same job level in the last organisation and are unable to see yourself grow.

You are eagerly waiting for the company to respond back, seeing your honesty, tenure with the company as well as all the hard work & efforts you had put in. You are very right to think that, but even after so much of hard work, why are you not getting a good hike or a promotion that you deserve.

However, there is no second thought about the fact that employer value those employees who are honest and hardworking. These factors are the key reasons for a strong relationship between the employer & its employee. But it is time to find out the actual reason, to find out what else is missing that is keeping you away from growth & rewards.

How can we fix this problem, how can we create those possibilities where your employer is happily recognising your efforts and rewarding you with a satisfactory hike or promotion?

Think for a while about Nokia's basic mobile with a keypad, a phone that has never disappointed me at all! These basic mobile phones are still selling at online stores & shops and have all basic calling, messaging & radio features. At the same time, these Nokia phones are reliable, durable, with good battery backup, and no matter how many more years you use them, they still have some value. Hardly a person who had ever used a Nokia basic phone will complain about its durability & long life. Isn't it? But do we use it anymore? A major number of the population have now shifted towards smartphones, technology has advanced and so have the trends.

We need to understand that there are only 2 things that market values today. One, ongoing trend should be followed,

secondly the regular upgrades, i.e. the new version of everything.

How can a Nokia basic mobile have the best sales when trends have changed, as upgraded versions of smartphones are being released almost every six months?

Our life growth depends upon this very simple principle; **we need to upgrade ourselves as per the trend to see outstanding growth.** Why I am emphasising on **outstanding growth** in specific because the basic versions are still in the market, as I just gave you an example about Nokia's basic keypad mobile phones ranging between 1300 INR to 3000 INR only, they are still in the market but not in high demand & trend anymore.

Time is running; technology is advancing every single second; every single skill has a new version in the market. We are moving towards an era where answers are given before we can raise a question.

Everything you scc around is now evolving too fast and I believe that a change like this which is way too fast, and too advanced can be troublesome for so many people who are not even aware of it. Automation of work is possible now; new machinery & technology has taken place for so many workers & professionals. My focus is not on what category of work or task we look around us, rather do a self-check on where we stand today. Competition is so cutthroat now that even the organisations are forced to merge these upgrades to match up with market trends, or else they will be left behind.

So, if you are reading this book with utmost sincerity & have determined to become an Action taker, then make sure you think about **UPGRADING yourself as soon as you read this.** Action takers will take notes in a mobile phone or will take a notepad or will simply add a reminder on the calendar to do research about what all skills you need to develop now as per the latest trends.

Proactive Approach: 4A

Promise yourself to spend 2 hours on the coming weekend for this research & your research should include the following:

1. Find the Job Titles that are available as per the industry you are in - note them somewhere.
2. Find the related skills in demand - as per the work industry & the Job titles you found above.
3. Search for online training & webinars that can add to your knowledge about this skill upgrade; all this should be done as per the industry you would love to work in or are currently working in.
4. Set up your mind - would you like to just enhance your skills through free online training, by doing a short-term certification, or if you want to actually get certified for a specific program that will provide you with a certified job title, or you want to go for an academic learning or higher studies.
5. The above step can only be understood when you clearly research about your work industry and its talent requirements.
6. Set up your budget - It is good if you already have savings in your bank and are ready to invest in skill development, or even if you do not have required funds as of now then don't worry the second last "Success principle 17" of this book will help you plan it in a better way! Check from your HR team or your reporting manager about company sponsorship if available

to complete your certification, most of the time employers have bonds where they sponsor the fee for your certification/ program that will add to the growth of the company as well. In such cases, employees are asked to stay with the company for a bond period of 2-3 years or more. These terms may vary from company to company.

Always remember, **an investment that is done for "Skill Development" will have the best ROI**. The only thing you need to do is to research extensively and get advice from someone senior in your profession. Stick to the trends & check for expert's opinion about the future requirements of the skill, program, or certification you are planning to do.

You should be confident & determined about the skill you are picking up and it should be an upgrade to your current profile, i.e. it should not deviate you from your long-term career plan.

How you can upgrade yourself to match the trend

Coming right to the point that an upgrade can be guaranteed only when we think about the following:

- **Skill Development.**
- **Following the latest trends with technology advancement.**
- **To understand our training needs very clearly.**
- **To have a Lifelong learning approach.**

It is very well said:

> *"Listen to the new, go with the new. I know you are afraid. In spite of the fear, go with the new, and your life will become richer and richer and you will be able one day to release your imprisoned splendour."*
>
> \- Osho

We can witness that the whole world & the work at the organisations are undergoing major change. Online training and skill development were already in trend, but it has reached its peak level right from the moment we stepped into the COVID-19 pandemic situation. Working remotely & getting unlimited training opportunities online is part of this new trend. Upgraded skills can contribute to better productivity and will open doors for extraordinary growth opportunities.

For understanding the type of skill you need, a little bit of research is must and guidance from a leader or a mentor will be good. This leader or mentor can be anywhere at your workplace or at your home. He/she should be someone who truly believes in you & the one you can trust the most. The steps should involve attending online training & webinar related to the work you are already doing. **There are multiple websites that are providing short term courses, online certification & training that can enhance your skill & knowledge ranging between beginner to specialised training & courses. Udemy, Pluralsight, Alison, Coursera are few examples from where you can start your research.**

WIN-WIN & No LOSS

Now, after the hard work & efforts you have put in to develop your skills, please try to maintain this pace of learning & keep following the trends.

Skills are worth learning only when they are applied, a skill that remains as a "learnt knowledge" is just a waste of time. That is why I emphasised on first doing extensive research, then picking up the right skill as an upgrade to your current profile.

- Inform your Talent Management team about the certification completed by you by sharing valid documents.
- Ask for opportunities & projects/work to apply these learned skills & knowledge, sooner or later your employer will add related work to your KRAs.
- Give some time to them to analyse your work & accordingly your increment percentage will be impacted; skills have already been upgraded & rest all depends upon your overall personality & positive attitude towards your job, your work ethics, and your relationship within your team.

Even after this in any worst scenario, if your employer fails to provide you with the desired growth opportunity that matches the current industrial trend & your capabilities, then it is time to move ahead.

This **decision of moving ahead is not very simple** and should not be taken in any hurry or just in need of a good salary hike. Please consider a couple of points before finalising this decision:

- If the employer expects your patience, then there must be some reason, any delay from considering your request can be due to reduced yearly turnover or fewer projects, fewer sales etc. In such scenarios, you must show faith in your organisation. The organisation has helped you to learn so many things and it is time for you to be patient & wait for them to consider your request.

- You must be 100% sure about the skills & certification done, and its market demand before you make a decision like this.
- Moving ahead should never mean to ditch your current employer, you must discuss & share your viewpoints with someone senior in the department and convey to them that you are looking for growth opportunities & motivation.
- If your decision is final, then you must fulfil all your responsibility as a leaving associate for e.g., serving a complete notice period, handing over all your work with complete honesty & with genuity so that a relationship built once stays strong forever.
- Your skill development should never be for just getting a monetary hike & so you must not get attracted toward any company who is ready to pay you your desired salary. You must go through reviews about the company, its culture, will they be really helping you to align your personal long-term career growth plan with the company's vision, do they really believe in work-life balance, do they have good policies in terms of employee welfare. These are random checks you need to do before you take this decision of separation from the current organisation as only money cannot satisfy or motivate you, the culture, the policies do matter along with salary & skills enhancement.

Imagine yourself as a badminton player, you pick up the

racket & start playing - but have you seen a player playing a tournament by just picking up a Bat, and start playing? He would not be allowed and would get eliminated from the tournament.

Like for playing cricket, you need to equip yourself with pads, gloves, helmet, bat etc. only then you are ready to bat, in the same way, you cannot fight with the employer to recognise your efforts only for the 1 skill that you are carrying with you!

Employment is surely like playing a cricket match. You must equip yourself with all required cricketing gears. You can only claim your success & check your worth when you have all of these:

- Correct attitude
- Self-motivation
- Honest & hardworking approach
- Adaptability
- **Skills Development**
- Long-term career focus
- Hunger to learn & grow
- Behaviour & professionalism
- Work ethics
- Healthy relationship with others

Why I have focused on SKILLS DEVELOPMENT a lot is just because that apart from the rest of the other factors, **this one factor has the power to make a swift change in your career growth map.** This can become the strongest reason to cover up for the rest of the weaker factors, but that should not mean you fool yourself by covering your mistakes, weaknesses & negative

AB quotient with this single factor! Being an employee, I can say this hundred more times that you need to strengthen each factor. **Skills development is one major part of it which has the quickest & immediate impact on your growth, but make sure you do not forget about the rest of the factors**. Just do it and nothing can stop you from getting the recognition for the work you do!

Success Principle 5

L-N-E Principle

The magical principle of life....

We understood this clearly by now that we need to upgrade our skills with changing trends. Changing your approach by reading these principles one after the other can only be possible if you are ready to implement these learnings & take actual actions.

Theories are written to take you to the point of initiation of **ACTIONS, and where your ACTIONS begin** the theory Ends & it gets converted into practical application and implementation. I am reminding you this again & again so that this fits deep inside your thoughts, inside your subconscious mind that it is NOW the time to see yourself grow by taking actions.

The power is in your hands, it is up to you & only you to convert any impossible thing into a possibility as impossible itself says I AM POSSIBLE, so just keep trying.

It would be incorrect to think that if you have upgraded your skills & knowledge, then your job is done! The L-N-E principle suggests that it is far from over!

L-N-E principle is to be implemented at the workplace as well in personal life.

"Once you Stop Learning, you Start dying".

- Albert Einstein

LEARNING - NEVER - ENDS.... i.e., The L-N-E principle.

We keep on learning lessons everyday, we keep on learning something new every now & then, it is just like a never-ending process.

So many of us lose the battle just by thinking that "I" know everything. It is very well said by Albert Einstein that once we stop learning, we start dying. It is because you want to change your life for the better & want to see growth at the career front which would result in a wonderful growth in your personal life too, it is because of this that you are reading so many articles to learn something new, you are reading this book, learning these principles and this is how you still feel alive. This is the energy of "Learning" as it keeps you alive; it keeps your mind functional.

What to learn?

Fad vs Trends

Fad or a trend are interchangeable terms, but if we go more in detail to understand it, **Fad** is something which becomes famous quickly, appears to be very attractive but probably does not last so long. **Trend** somehow has a different impact; it grows gradually and we have noticed the trend keeps on changing and is still connected to its origin point. Do not get attracted by fads during this process as they become popular very fast but may fade away easily in a short span of period. We should follow the **trend that has a visible revision pattern over the last few years.**

The Deletion

I request you to first delete this phrase from your life dictionary that "I know everything"!

Let us remove it permanently from our brains in just 3….2...1… seconds...That is it! Was it very tough for you to accept that no one can know "everything", there is always something, a little out of plenty that still needs to be learnt, to be explored, to be seen and to be experienced! There is no purpose in our life any further if we know everything & are knowledgeable about everything we see hear or experience.

Never be 100% Satisfied with yourself

The Saga is not the end.

Saga, i.e. a long story of heroic achievement, and just like you, I too had a Saga to share about my struggles, how I overcame it & what achievements I accomplished in my life. Just a metaphor I have taken here to explain to my readers that each one of us has our own saga about how hard we had worked & performed to get to this place. I am sure that you have put in enormous efforts in life and you expect now that your hard work pays off.

I always appreciate myself for being an optimistic person who was able to fight so many challenges in life with a smile, but **I never allowed my victories to get to my head.**

Just relating to the fact that the moment we will be satisfied with our success & victories, that will be the moment we can become snobbish about our own victories & achievements in life, we lose the essence of every single victory we achieved so far!

I want to change for myself, not for others. My hard work & actions will directly affect my life, not anyone else's life. I cannot keep lauding myself every now & then for what I have achieved as this makes us dull & inactive.

I know this may seem a little harsh to you to read, but I am sharing this with my own experience & how it can really affect our productivity at the workplace as well in personal life. I was so happy to admire my achievements, about the victories I had in my life that I literally forgot about the future for a moment!

This realisation came to me when I joined Nichiren Buddhism, an amazing life-changing philosophy & a kind of meditation/chanting technique to dig out our highest potentials. This introspection was like a blast in my head!

Maybe what I realised through introspection is that those efforts & struggles, those achievements of getting an extra incentive for my good work, those rewards & promotions I got at my job have now become a "past", and they will undoubtedly keep on reaping fruits.

Once these fruits are consumed by us, not so quickly but gradually the taste of these fruits will be forgotten by our tongue and to keep having the same old sweet taste of these fruits, we must keep planting new trees, we must keep working hard, **we must keep learning!**

Admiring our own success, feeling 100% satisfied with ourselves at any level & taking no further actions will make us INACTIVE.

Sit for a while, introspect, think about your saga moments in your mind, see what you have achieved so far, feel happy about the skill developments, latest certifications/degree attained recently but **never be 100% satisfied** with all this. There is always a scope for improvement or to learn something more even when we get expertise in a particular area or subject.

Merge L-N-E principle in your daily habits for exceptional results!

Take a pen and paper or make notes on your mobile:

What are the first 5 tasks you perform on your mobile phone when you get up in the morning and check it at the start of the day?

For example:

If you are too fond of mobile phones, then before getting up from the bed you check your mobile phone for new messages and the push-notifications from social media seize the first few most precious minutes of your day! Or in some cases, you are not very fond of mobile phones; you close the alarm on your mobile phone, then quickly check the messages, notifications, and read the news headlines etc. before you start your day. Or in some more amazing cases, you close the alarm and look at the time. You get up, brush your teeth or drink water, do some exercise, and start your day. The routine can vary from person to person.

After you get up, the first five things you do can be these or any other; I just want you to read these & relate it with those first few activities you do when you get up in the morning:

You got up in the morning and then right after you open your eyes:

1. You check all social media notifications & respond to them, like or dislike the posts, wish someone their birthdays etc. **or**
2. You hardly engage yourself in liking, disliking the post on social media but keep scrolling on to the screen from your favourite social media account, a quick glance on some pictures, videos etc. **or/and**
3. Revert to important messages or any missed call **followed by/ or**
4. Reading the news headlines or checking any work-related update **or**
5. You have a personal "To Do" task list on your mobile phone, you update it & remind yourself about the planned tasks for the day.

You can pick from the above options or can think of an answer in your own way.

The success of your day that is ahead depends upon how good you had spent your first 30 minutes right after you woke up. These first 30 minutes can affect the productivity of the next 23.5 hours of your day.

Let us not think about when we went to sleep as you may have worked late into the night, or you may have responsibilities at home. The point is not about when do we roll out of our beds, but how do we spend our first 30 minutes as soon as we open our eyes in the morning.

So many people spend half of their time scrolling up & down

on Social Media and if you are really spending first 30 minutes of the day by checking text messages, immediately responding to calls, responding to the social media notification then let me tell you, **this world, these people on the social media have grabbed most of your attention. Indirectly and unintentionally, they have become the most major reason for you not getting desired growth in your own life.**

Where were you?

Think for a while; you are spending your precious time looking at another person's life, that too this is the first thing you do in the morning. Or even if you do not have any such attraction towards social media, you still spend the first 30 minutes of your day responding back to messages that are sent by someone, calls that are done by someone, emails that are sent by someone and so on...

In total, you started your day with others & ended your day for others! **Where were you in all this chaos?** Let us go by a scientific theory about this.

Scientifically it has been said that when we first wake up, our brain operates at around 10.5 waves per second and this ranges from 8.0 to 13.0 Hz cycles per second. This phase is also known as the alpha stage when our subconscious mind is in the best mode to absorb & soak whatever is fed to it.

So now you can clearly imagine what all your subconscious mind has absorbed so far. Make sure not to check your social media account, emails, messages when you wake up in the morning.

It is your day; no one is going to spend that in place of you, the challenges are yours, the success & failures are only yours.

The result will only shake hands with you. Start your day by changing yourself completely for these first 30 minutes as it is the most precious & effective time to think & grow fast.

Tomorrow whenever you wake up, start your first 30 minutes like this & believe me in just a couple of days you will be a totally changed personality, i.e. a more focussed & optimistic person who believes in himself or herself to accomplish desired goals.

The only condition you need to follow is to NOT touch your mobile phones during these first 30 minutes, not even looking at the screen to see the notifications that are popping up.

Proactive Approach: 5A

- After getting up, sit peacefully on your bed, close your eyes and with a smile on your face think about 3 things of your life for which you feel blessed, any 3 things that make you happy and have a sense of gratitude in your thoughts. Spend 2-3 minutes on this.
- Now for the next 5 minutes just sit, focus on your breathing with closed eyes, notice how the air goes In, how it goes out from your nose, you do not have to intentionally pull in or throw out the air from your nose, just monitor your breathing for 5 minutes. Feel relaxed and happy.

- For the next 10 minutes your eyes remain closed, now think about your Goals, these goals should be fixed in advance and should be written somewhere. You can also pick up some of the best success & growth-related "affirmations". Now read them first to yourself from the notes where you have written these affirmations and goals that are to be achieved. Now as your subconscious mind is absorbing the best of the information during these first 30 mins, **visualise the future's best version of "you" that you want to become, visualise a rich yet happy person that is you, visualise that these Goals have already been achieved by you & feel happy about it.** Think about what actions you are taking to get to this best version of yours.
- For the Next 5 minutes, open your eyes, focus upon any major thing you had planned for today without looking at your mobile phone, think about any pending tasks of yesterday, think where you left your work yesterday. Think about what research you can do about attending any online webinar or training sessions that can add to your learning process.
- After this, you can get up from the bed, take a small walk, drink a glass of water, or start your workout or start following your basic routine brimming with energy & joy. Read something knowledgeable, go through newspaper headlines, if you do not do exercise, then walk for a few moments, etc.

During these first 30 minutes that you will spend with yourself, make sure that you do not check any text message, missed calls and notification from social media. **Dedicate these first 30 minutes purely to yourself** to tap the highest potential and to maximise your productivity at work.

The world can wait for 30 minutes, but your precious time & success cannot wait for you to enjoy its benefits.

Time to merge L-N-E principle with this routine, you must be thinking about putting extra efforts for it.

Now when you make the first 30 minutes this much focussed then your subconscious mind starts acting in the same manner, the dreams, the visualisation which you have each day increases the hunger of your brain to learn something new that adds value to this goal.

Ask yourself what I should be doing to convert this visualisation of rich & happy me into reality. Keep working hard in that direction and see the magic!

You will be transformed into a keen learner if you genuinely understand the magical principles of "Skill Development," i.e. to upgrade yourself with latest trends & market demands and by following this magical key to success, i.e. the "L-N-E success principle."

By now, you must be a transformed person with a completely new fresh approach towards learning. A transformation is nothing but your desire to learn more, your desire to know more about your current profile and towards the value-adding skills, which will surely result in maximising your productivity at the workplace.

Now let's finetune our learning habits by changing a couple of more approaches to develop a strong L-N-E habit that can really help us to transform better.

Do not be ashamed to ask!

The situation will come when while working as a team, you will encounter many issues & you would want to work on a problem together as a team. Your peers & subordinates are to be respected for the work they do for you. Yes, it is part of their job, but just by showing gratitude & appreciating them, you can make their job easy & valuable.

Sometimes our subordinate knows a better solution, a better formula, a better code, a better process, or a better technique to complete a task. But as we are not ready to listen to them, or maybe we do not have confidence in them, we skip learning something new and better.

Even if you are working individually and know a person around you who is 1 or 2 levels lower as per the organisational hierarchy, then it does not mean you cannot ask for help, solution & suggestion from him/her. Always be ready to absorb the knowledge from wherever it is coming, you should not think about the designation, experience & age of that person.

I always remind myself the beautiful & meaningful lines said by one of the best poets from history, Abdul Rahim Khan-I-Khanan, he said:

रहिमन देखि बड़ेन को, लघु न दीजिए डारि
जहां काम आवे सुई, कहा करे तरवारि

English translation to this:

"Never despise the little one on seeing the big one,
For where a needle comes to use, of what use is a sword?"

I read this lyrical verse when I was in school and this got imprinted in my mind since then, I am already amazed by the sense of wisdom oozing out of this verse. Let us not have the titles of senior or junior in our minds, do not let your designation or profile become a hindrance in your path of learning and growth.

You should not be ashamed of something that can expand your knowledge.

The time & place to apply this L-N-E principle

Can you think of the time & place that is best to apply your knowledge & to learn something new from others? Think about it for a few second.! Got any answers?

Please be aware that **there is no specific time & place to apply the L-N-E principle.** How can we decide that it is time to learn something? Learning is a never-ending process and you should make it your habit. You can learn anywhere anytime & can apply this knowledge as per the requirement.

Other than the skills development & certification you have done or are planning to do, you should keep checking and attending regular training, webinar & workshops related to your profile & work. Visualising about the Rich & Successful happy "YOU" daily in the morning during the first 30 minutes of the day will align your knowledge with this Goal achievement.

You will be amazed to see the mystical power of the subconscious mind & Universe's response towards it. Unlimited windows of opportunities one after the other will be opened for you, one can see these opportunities coming towards only when he/she spends quality time with him/herself & with the subconscious mind. I request my readers without giving it a second thought & try this by yourself. Give yourself sufficient time & see phenomenal results.

Be a Good SPEAKER but first a Superb LISTENER!

I still remember those days when I used to be the most annoying person in the past who wanted to explain everything, who used to defend herself for any question asked, for the critical feedback received by the manager, or for my mistakes. Without listening much, I used to defend myself. As a speaker, I always had a hurry to put my point in front of others.

I feel this may be due to my fears of getting trapped into any wrong conclusions that were to be reached; I always have this anxiety that if I would not speak & share this factor, then the decision may come out to be something different.

I can literally laugh at myself now thinking about the kind of eagerness I had for speaking in front of others. I changed this approach years ago when my friends started to take advice from me on relationships, career and about the challenges they face in personal life.

We can only learn about something when we develop the habit of listening first & then decide to speak. This habit cannot be developed so easily, but with practice, we can become a Superb listener.

I had to tell myself that we cannot change others & their decisions; we must see the possible "change" we can bring into ourselves to get the best possible outcome.

This feeling of not getting impatient & stressed has helped me to transform myself completely and when we change then the world itself appears different to us. How does it really matter if "they" change for you or if their opinion changes for you!

So, I stopped defending myself on the criticism I heard; I stopped defending myself on the mistakes that were shared with me. I kept on learning from the people around me. This never meant that I agreed to the invalid blames during arguments, but as I already mentioned, I was so ready to learn & accept things that I was able to present the reality in front of others without defending myself with words.

"Education is the ability to listen to almost anything without losing your temper or self-confidence."

- Robert Frost

I am one live example for you. Today I can listen to new ideas, suggestions, feedback, complaints calmly without losing the temper & I always try to be a good listener. As a person who believes in the small yet strongest word "CHANGE" I am always happy to incorporate those suggestions, ideas & feedback into my own life, **but only after doing the required research & by applying the best possible self-wisdom**. There is no harm to learn & grasp anytime, anywhere no matter from where the knowledge is showered, just stand beneath this shower of "knowledge, education & wisdom, raise your hands, open up your mind and let your mind absorb the best of it, **throwing the negatives out of your mind".**

Closing with a wonderful quote by Leonardo da Vinci, that the only action that has no side effect is learning.

"Learning never exhausts the mind."

- Leonardo da Vinci

Success Principle 6

The thin line between politeness & being speechless

Which one are you?

Do people take you for granted because you are too polite?

Or

Do people avoid you because you are not at all polite?

Both are harmful and may hinder our career growth. Change of approach is required to relate between these two terms - **Politeness vs Harshness.** As we are Human Beings, we cannot eliminate any one of the two completely from our existence. Both these traits are in us when one is Active, the other one automatically gets deactivated, i.e. into the dormant state.

As a matter of fact, we need to let the "politeness" remain in ACTIVE MODE leaving behind harshness. This is one beautiful principle that can also be applied in personal life, but when we are at a place where we follow guidelines, rules & policies, we are bound to be polite & are bound to throw our harshness, short temperedness outside the office doors.

Let us keep ourselves in these scenarios and find where we currently are. I personally love to imagine myself in various scenarios as this really helps me to find the best version of me within a few minutes after an introspection.

These are just the scenarios, not to be considered as a trait of you or someone else's. Let us try to imagine hypothetically if you are among one of these, then what impression you are giving to your co-workers:

If you are too polite:

- You are very polite, always smile & say yes to everything while you are at your workplace, because of which people do not take you and your suggestions seriously at all, maybe they think you are buttering them? Or they think you are not able to understand the criticality of the situations.? Or are you an easy target to bully? or
- Maybe your 24*7 smiling habits & very soft polite tone make others feel powerful enough that they are taking advantage of you? or
- You are too polite to handle arguments and you end up being quiet even when you were expected to speak, you are so tender-hearted that during arguments your mind becomes blank and people find you speechless? or
- You are so polite that even if you want to put your point forward, your voice is not heard during the meeting, group discussion & arguments?

Just opposite to the above scenarios,

Imagine yourself if you are too harsh & short-tempered:

- You try to be nice to everyone with your polite tone but somehow unable to handle mistakes done by any team members, feedbacks or arguments given to you and you lose all your temper? People avoid you because you have a harsh tone, not every time but sometimes? Or

- You try to be patient, but end up shouting at people for the Work "Not Done Yet"? Or
- You try to stay calm but unable to handle illogical blames & miscommunications within the team and you end up speaking harshly with someone or with anyone who comes in your way? Or
- You want to enjoy the power & the authorities given to you. Your tone might appear normal to you while you talk, but it may sound harsh & unacceptable to others because of your senior profile?

Think............ Think.............. and Think.........!

Then take a deep breath, nobody is going to judge you here, this is your space, your book, your imagination & your scenarios. Be honest with yourself and try to introspect a little. Peep a little inside your heart & think about a couple of recent interactions you had with your team or with any individual, no matter what department or profile it was, it may be a client, any stakeholder, any visitor or even the housekeeping staff.

Just go back in time, I want you to recall the last 3 interactions that had some impact either on you or the other person? We always know the truth subconsciously so you cannot skip this part by saying I cannot think of it, or I do not know anything about it.

So, be true to yourself and think! It is ok if you are not perfect and realise something odd about yourself. And it is great if you are already doing well as per the scenarios mentioned above.

Do not get confused here by considering "politeness" as a negative impression when characterised "too much" in front of others. Yes, not being polite is still ok **but being harsh in your tone is something nobody will like at your workplace.**

If we go by theory & definitions, then politeness falls under the category of good manners or etiquettes which we reflect in our speech practically, i.e., we are able to express our thoughts & intentions politely without offending the other person.

As I already told you at the beginning that CHANGE of APPROACH is to think broadly & to think a step ahead, so we are not at all referring to these general polite terms, like "Thank you", "Sorry", Yes sir," "No sir," or "Yes ma'am," "No ma'am", "Please," "May I,", "You're Welcome," "Excuse Me," "Pardon Me. etc. the list is long.

These phrases to me are the very basic courtesy or polite words that we use while showing respect to the person in front of us and if you have correctly understood the AB principle by now, then these etiquettes will automatically get developed by having a positive AB Quotient, i.e. your overall attitude & behaviour toward others.

To think a step ahead means to change something that is not under your surveillance until now, and you can start monitoring yourself for this so that this change can have a fantabulous impact on you & the people around you. Believe me, if you change yourself to pull out the "The Best Version" of you, then people around you will be forced mystically or with logical reasons to change themselves with you for good.

They will feel so free & comfortable in your presence that you will always be protected from manipulations, politics at office and arguments. Be a turtle, not a rabbit, little slow but do keep on moving steadily without stopping in between the career roadmap you have planned for yourself.

We will learn to maintain a balance between "I am polite Vs I am too polite". We are also going to understand this act of "extreme politeness" can attract the act of "speechlessness".

Too polite to handle arguments

As we understand that being a good listener will help us build a strong bond within the team. It is also good to learn about the other person's ideas & suggestions before presenting your views on the topic.

Sometimes we are good at listening but too polite at times during critical arguments & group discussions and thus are not able to convey the correct message or statement that supports our argument. This does not mean that you should fight or always try to win the arguments, but when it is about your work & your team, then you must learn to put your point in front of others in such a way that no one gets offended. You don't need to dominate the conversation, nor do you need to be so polite that it appears that you cannot put your point when needed.

There is this **thin line between too much politeness and speechlessness;** we can easily sink into speechlessness when we try to be extremely polite. Again, we are not trying to be rude at all in any circumstance whatever it may be; we must remain calm and polite. Politeness as a reaction & etiquette should be balanced well.

Some people being too polite & helping that they are unable to say "NO", and some on the other side become so rude for any extra efforts they take for others if they are not able to bear any benefits for "self" in return. They act just in accord with the barter system; they can only make efforts for others if the work provides them with some credit, recognition, or reward for it.

The Three Levels Voice Tone Model: 6A

Let us understand the basics by learning "The Three Levels Voice Tone Model" mentioned below; we can visualise ourselves at any level as per our current situation.

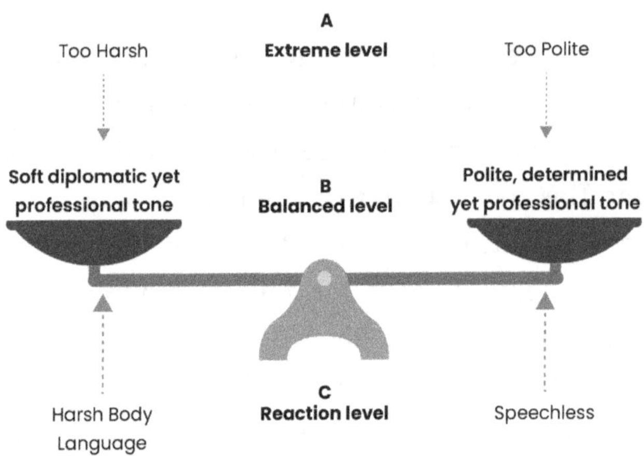

1. Extreme Level A (Unbalanced state) - This is the extreme level, where the interaction between 2 members or more than 2 members can **reflect either a harsh tone or too polite tone.** Yes, the second one, i.e. too polite, is a "great to have" characteristic in the human body & is very tough to achieve. **But**

I personally feel that anything done in excess can be harmful. We already read above what people can think or what scenarios we can face if the tone is Too Harsh or Too polite.

2. Target Level B (Balanced state)- This is the place where maybe you already are, if not, then this should be your target level.

Two different types of change of approaches are required here:

- To not use your authority at work ***by cutting down the harshness from the tone.***
- On the other hand, to be able to convey your message professionally yet confidently ***by avoiding the act of speechlessness.***

If we maintain the balance while standing at level B (as per the model 6A), you can understand that even the critical message can be conveyed **softly yet diplomatically without reflecting the harsh tone**, i.e. no matter how much angry you are at any particular situation or how much rudely you want to talk to someone because of his/her mistakes, because of fewer sales this month, because of incorrect work, or delay in the work submission or for having so many client's concerns or complaints etc.

You should **STAY at level B,** to tell the concerned party about the mistake, concern or issues while **maintaining a soft tone with a diplomatic speech yet confident enough** to convey the right message. This is how both the parties can maintain their pace at work professionally without getting distracted due to emotional & mental disturbance. This disturbance is caused generally after any argument due to harsh tone or due to negative AB quotients of either of the parties.

Vice versa, no matter how much you want a task to be completed, no matter how much you need to please the second person, or no matter how much neutral you are while assessing other's mistakes related to work, but you should not avoid all the mistakes, any misbehaviour, or the critical allegation against you & your team. Sometimes you need to **speak up and convey the right message at the right time**. While staying at **level B,** not going very easy or extremely polite in critical situations, **you must maintain a normal polite tone yet determined & confident tone so that you can put your point forward.**

Your tone should never leave any statement unclear for the other person neither it should be offensive for the person in front of you, or else you will fail to achieve the purpose of this interaction.

Do not stay completely neutral against questions that have been asked from you, or for the complaints that you have received or for the concerns that you may have from someone within the team or outside the team.

If we try, we can simply put the critical point forward without ending up being speechless. This thin line between extremely polite & speechlessness **can be erased permanently** if you **focus on level B, be more determined by using a more balanced polite and confident tone at work.**

Nevertheless, you can use the same principle in your personal life as well, be it your family members, friends, or any unknown person, always stay at level B to handle arguments or any differing thoughts. It is very normal to have varying thoughts; we just need to focus on the conclusion that should be obtained with a polite, determined, yet confident tone.

3. Reaction Level C (Unbalanced state): The level of **"reaction"** where we do not use words, nor do we even want to express our message by using words. We feel hopeless that the other person cannot or will not be able to understand our point.

A situation where our body language can reflect what we feel as we do not want to speak, but we are angry or furious about something and our body language is very rude & unwelcoming.

For example, we avoid eye contact, sit with crossed arms and frowning expressions, and have a poor sitting posture etc.

In case of extreme politeness, body language can portray different gestures, for example: Over smiling to hide our confusion behind the inability to express our message clearly, breathing heavily due to nervousness or anxiety, nodding head too frequently to give our agreement on any or everything the other person says as we are unable to express our own thoughts correctly.

This level C is the Silent illustration of Level A where without speech, our body language & gestures depict our intentions directly or indirectly. If you want to perform well & would like to be a top performer at work, these small actions & reactions are very important to be balanced. This adds to our overall personality & career growth.

To remain at Level B and to communicate effectively you must practice the following during meetings, presentation, critical arguments, group discussions or during the planning meetings etc. where various types of ideas & thoughts can be shared.

Proactive Approach: 6B

To communicate effectively by remaining at Level B

- **Step 1. Prepare yourself before the time** - Before the meeting understand the purpose of the meeting very clearly, check the agenda or check with the concerned members (any 1 or 2) the requirements & purpose of the meeting so that you can do some research well in advance & know what all points you need to share. It will help you to remain confident & calm throughout the discussion.

- **Step 2. Focus on your Body language & tone**- Our body language and tone can impact the conversation, let us become a good listener and allow the representatives & meeting coordinators to share their points first. Sit straight and always make proper eye contact, keep calm, be confident. **Keep reminding yourself that you are ready to convey your point effectively without changing your tone by getting too harsh or too polite.** A smiling confident expression will work fine, but you should be determined to share your decision or key points that you had prepared before the meeting.

- **Step 3. Let others complete their conversation:** if you notice any 2 people already discussing some points then do not get over-excited and anxious to jump in between the conversation to share your prepared points of conflicting opinions on the topic. It is better to remain silent when 2-3 members are discussing something specific that does not require your involvement at this moment. Wait for the right time & seek consent to add a point while the conversation is going on, you must do it on time before the decisions are finalised else you might not agree to the final result.

For example: If anyone from the meeting group completes his/her point and takes a pause, you should politely yet confidently request them like so:

"Sir, would you mind if I add something here..."

or

"Mam, I would like to add something here..."

or

"Please allow me to share some key highlights related to the concern we are referring to here..."

These kinds of statements should provide you with a start and this is how you can get involved in the ongoing discussion without interrupting anyone. **Timing is everything,** so find the best time when you need to get involved in any discussion or argument.

In case you are the main lead & representative for the particular topic, which is going to be discussed at the meeting, then listen to the other party first. Note down the differences in opinions. Use the effective communication tools through correct body language & tone to convey your ideas on it without offending any of the party or member.

- **Step 4. Agreements from all the parties or members:** At the end, whatever decision is taken, it is very important that you recapitulate the key points to confirm upon the final decision or agreed points. Allow the meeting representative to conclude the decision, or if by chance it is missed, then you can yourself conclude the discussion point by taking final agreements from all the parties.

- **Step 5. Written communication is POWER:** Whatever discussion is done during the meeting, make sure the written records are maintained about the agreed points for any future reference. You must send over an e-mail the summary of what has been discussed or decided by the concerned parties. This information can be retrieved anytime in future; it can also help in informing those members who had missed the meeting due to any unforeseen reason.
- **Step 6. The Follow up:** The general points discussed at the meeting can be shared in a summary on e-mail but if there is any acceptance that is pending from any of the parties then make sure to follow up until you get the acknowledgement on e-mail.

Success Principle 7

The presentation of "ME."

Let us further do a check upon our overall presentation in front of others, our personality, conduct & communication skills followed by the business writing.

The half journey

You want to take a leap, a high jump, what if someone tells you that the quickest way to complete your half journey on a career map **depends upon the presentation of "you" and your personality.**

Whatever you have read so far, all the changes of approach that I am requesting here are part of various types of competencies that add value to your KRA's. It can be named differently in different organisations. Ultimately, we must understand that whatever we do at the workplace, how we do, when we do, where we do, all these questions when answered or analysed for an individual becomes his/her performance parameters and on the basis of this a person is monitored, rewarded and recognised.

"What we do"- The task & the work that has been assigned to us comes under this.

"How we do" - AB quotient if we accept or reject the work, or our attitude for accomplishing a task, or if we learn something from what we do.

"When we do" - Includes the work timings, i.e. ETA (a term used to measure the expected time of completion of any work), How good are we able to plan our work in a way that we abide by the work-life balance requirements.

Evaluation of these questions can be counted under technical competencies & what are we doing to accomplish these competencies as per the employer's requirement.

Other than these parameters, the weightage is given to individual competencies that include - How the employee presents himself in front of the manager, team, stakeholders & clients or what is the employee's AB quotient, how good is the employee at learning and implementation etc.

Let us understand it through this scenario:

As per the scenario, we have this organisation ABC Pvt. Ltd. that has one of the best architect designers and they have a strong presence in the market. The technical team is very efficient in delivering quality work on time and all its clients are very happy with the work.

Start thinking hypothetically now!

They have this associate, **Mr. Rajat,** working as the architectural designer, he is so dedicated to his work that no one can compete with the designs he creates and most of the time the client finalises his created design without suggesting a lot of changes. This confirms that the designer has a strong grip on his technical skills. The client's site is in France.

Mr. Rajat had to never visit the client or even be required to communicate a lot with clients. Whatever work he submits, he submits to the team lead! Also, the employer is aware of his weak areas, i.e. that he needs to really work upon individual competencies that we discussed above. However, because of his strong work efficiency, they ignored a lot of things, like his presentation, personality, and overall conduct. From the employer's side, Mr. Rajat had always received rewards & recognition.

As a reader, do focus on this scenario very carefully as a major part of this story is about to get revealed, and you will understand how personality, presentation and effective communication help us to fast track our career growth.

Mr. Rajat is not much but a little bit of an introvert yet he does not want to interact a lot, he understands the software well & can work on the most critical design models, but he needs to work on his communication skills, he never wanted to present his work to the client himself. Maybe he thinks his communication & presentation skills are not very effective? He wants to save himself from any embarrassment and would like to enjoy the **rewards he is getting only based on his technical competencies.**

His personality and low confidence make him less powerful in front of other associates even when he is the most valued employee because of his habit to upgrade his skills every now & then to keep himself up to date to the current market trends. **The client has loved his work & wants to invite him to the client location, i.e. France, which is undoubtedly a great opportunity for any employee.**

Now, will the employee be sending him to France as he

may need to handle the whole project design individually & has to closely interact with the client. How will Mr. Rajat be able to cope up with this problem? Has he ever thought that these competencies can also become a hindrance in his growth as this opportunity is so amazing & huge that it can transform his career growth graph completely?

Now the question which you need to answer here is, who is becoming the hindrance & who can remove the hindrance that is blocking your success roadmap?

Is it so easy for the organisation to decide that Mr. Rajat should be sent to France only based on his technical skills? However, he is not very interactive, expressive, weak at his communication & needs to really work on his personality. You already know the answer by now.

Every single individual at any organisation represents it EQUALLY; you cannot distinguish this by profile, designation & hierarchy.

It really does not matter whether you are a front office executive, whether you represent a manufacturing department, research department, shared services, engineering department, or are a cook in a hotel who works behind the scenes. **You never know from where, when & how the opportunity might knock your door!**

The only thing that we can do here is to keep upgrading our skills and practise them to convert the acquired knowledge into applied knowledge and **along with this we need to strictly work upon our individual competencies,** i.e. the presentation of "Me".

The way we talk, the way we balance our AB quotient, how effective our communication skills are, all these small-small knacks can make a huge difference. These knacks which I call the other half of the required skills (other than your learnt/technical skills) can majorly crank up the career growth pace.

To ensure you never face a roadblock in the middle of your career growth map, let us try to build a strong personality and become more expressive professionally. **Let us count these skills amongst the most influential skills of the current market, i.e., our communication, presentation, and personality.**

A good personality is not only wearing the best outfit!

A donkey if given some good clothes, formal shoes and a tie, cannot impress us at all. Do you agree? The correct **proportion of required skills in an individual** is very important, which ultimately gives birth to a new, fully skilled employee who has expertise in all the areas. So, **the dumbest person with a poor brain & IQ can have a very good personality** & can fool anybody who needs not to interact with this person.

Personality should reflect Person's Originality, i.e. when it is said that this person's personality is quite good, then that means he is good at his **interactions, presentation**, his **agreeableness, attentiveness, openness** and his **levels of tolerance** in stressful situations. These are a few traits that, when consolidated, makes a perfect personality.

There are reasons why we do not wear party dresses daily on a working day and there are specific dress codes as per various occasions.

The dress codes are strictly followed as per industry, for

an example if you work in a hotel then you cannot ignore the specific guidelines mentioned for the dress code as it is all about the customer who is stepping into the hotel. Not only this, but because of strict hygiene maintenance policies in the hospitality industry, the backend staff is bound to follow each & every guideline very seriously.

On the opposite to this many IT companies that are away from the client's location has a very cool, stress-free working atmosphere, they need the best code, best on-time project delivery, a very strong agile business model etc.

So, when the client is abroad, the guidelines are kept flexible and it may sometimes be ignored if employees are coming in casuals. The scenario is completely different when the client visits the office location and the employees follow a formal dress code because then it really does not matter if the engineer prefers a relaxed working environment or does not want to imprison himself into formal clothing.

Few people carry a wonderful attractive personality all the time, **they do not need the client to visit them daily, or any stakeholder to check upon their dress code or their overall personality.** These people are the best resources at any organisation who do not need any trigger or factor to maintain their personality & their presentation in front of the stakeholders/ clients or other team members.

These are self-motivated, happy people who are always good at balancing AB quotient, LNE principle as well as are focused on their skills development with changing trends. They work honestly for the organisation and strongly believe that **someone**

who can best represent the organisation is "its employees" and that they would easily get noticed in the crowd of thousands of people because of their strong personality.

The Aura that we carry!

You will be able to re-energies your personality instantly by wearing your best outfits in the office. We create an aura with our gesture, communication, presentation, and neat clothing.

Moreover, you must "LOVE YOURSELF" and your own personality before it is noticed or judged by someone else. You feel so positively energetic when you start your day by seeing a smartly dressed, hygienic person in the mirror. You become a channel of happy, positive energy with your dressing and conduct!

So, even when your organisation does not follow any dress code, still take time out for shopping after every 4-6 months for buying some new formal/semi-formal clothes for daily wear. Do you know why? Neat & clean clothes carry so much of good vibes, we feel more confident and happier to meet someone. ***Try this and you will love yourself!***

Opportunity, if available, should not be allowed to easily escape without providing the exposure & recognition that you deserve in life. Want to be that kind of employee who always stands under the spotlight throughout his/her career?

Then always remember that not a single factor or principle has to be avoided here for changing your approach,.i.e. before expecting the world to change for you, as we need to first work upon ourselves.

When we focus upon our overall growth & development, automatically, we can dig out our highest work potential & strengths. Of course, this magic of self-belief & meeting the best version of "I" can only be witnessed with discipline and by smartly doing the hard work. We must spend time with ourselves for each factor we just discussed so far & would be discussing in upcoming sections.

Let us recall quickly what we have learnt:

Morning 20 minutes meditation technique, Positive attitude & behaviour model, maintaining the tone, most importantly your skill development & upgradation as per latest market trends so that the new version of yours can easily be seen. Work on your soft skills, align your career goal with that of the organisation to see fast career growth and finally focus on your personality & your presentation skills.

You know why I recall all these points after every 1-2 sections because it requires a "change of approach", "change of mindset" and to completely renew our vision & goals. All of this can be done with strong determination & discipline. This is easy to achieve, but only when you are mentally and psychologically ready to visualise the best version of yours in the near future, and only when you start believing in yourself.

You can trust me and so many other authors or success coaches, entrepreneurs, successful leaders who have ever talked about these changes. You must believe in this small yet powerful word "CHANGE" that changes the way we think, our adaptability, our determination, our hunger for success which really can **affect**

the speed with which our career graph will move.

Promise yourself that from now on, you are a completely different person & that you are ready for inculcating these changes to see remarkable results in your career.

Your personality should match the level of your knowledge.

So now when you believe in yourself, you must be sure that both factors are achievable: a good personality & the knowledge (skills). Initially, your personality can be judged by your clothing & to follow the dress code is a very good practice. But the rest of the impression you leave on someone is by your communication skills, knowledge & the tone.

We already understood in detail, about skill development techniques & how it should be developed. Let us follow a couple of things to develop a strong personality, or to add onto our existing strong personality:

- If you truly **believe in yourself and your skills,** then you will always feel confident about yourself. Avoid being overconfident because of your skills & knowledge; let us just stick to "self-confidence" as this is a major part of your personality. When we are confident, it is reflected in our personality. **A weak personality always has self-doubt & worries.**

So, we have this key to learning that really boosts our self-confidence. You will be able to involve yourself in the most critical tasks and research with confidence.

- **Refusal without being offensive** - From the beginning, we are learning about how to accept, how to learn, how to take things positively, how to be ready to listen, & then speak. **This never meant that every answer should be given with a "Yes"** even when you are not in a situation to say "yes".

Also, when we say that we need to build a strong positive, decent personality, and need to balance our tone, and keep our gestures remarkable, then **your "NO" or disagreement should be in such a way that it never offends the other person.**

I agree that, in rare cases, even the best polite refusal becomes offensive if the second person only wanted to hear your answer in agreement. It is ok to disagree sometimes, as we do not want to develop a fake personality by saying "yes" all the time.

We cannot disagree with someone just to run away from our responsibilities, that is a really bad sign while working at any organisation.

Let us understand with some examples of how to share our disagreement or to say "No":

Sentence 1 - It is **impossible** for us to initiate the replacement for this order.

Sentence 2 - I am sorry **we are unable** to initiate the replacement for this order.

By using this term "impossible," we are showing our anxiety & low self-esteem, rather than genuinely feeling sorry for not being able to provide the service due to organisation terms & conditions or due to any policy.

Proactive Approach: 7A

If someone asks for your help & you are unable to provide your support or need to disagree to any statement, then you can start your sentence by saying:

- I am honoured, but I cannot at this moment……
- I am sorry, I have a couple of other commitments…
- Unfortunately, now is not a good time for it…
- I am sorry, I am in the middle of something very important at this moment...
- Thank you, it sounds amazing, but can I join next time?...

We have **shared disagreement** in every sentence that is mentioned above, **yet we are trying not to be offensive.**

We need to avoid using such statements, i.e. it will sound offensive when we are trying to throw our stress upon the other person like so:

- I do not have time for all this...
- Please leave me alone with my work. I need to submit this work asap...
- Please No! I just cannot.
- How can you even ask this from me?...
- That is not my job, do it yourself...
- Absolutely No!...

Also, there are several trainings & short-term courses, online applications for learning business communication for handling formal group discussions & for your personality development.

If you love to invest money, then this will be your best investment if you feel you need a little assistance or help in polishing your existing business communication. Your tone can be judged not only when you speak, but while writing e-mails also, your tone can easily be sensed by the reader.

Be confident of what you are writing, your e-mail or message should reflect sincerity, avoid using too authoritative or harsh tone in e-mails & messages. Figure out the areas wherein your e-mail, the emphasis should be given and where subordination is required. If you want to emphasise on any negative point, then start by stressing on some positive points and then gradually shift towards the area of improvements.

All you need is to spend time with yourself, do a little research and there is almost everything that is available online for enhancing the skills you are looking to develop in yourself.

This book will surely lead you to unlimited possibilities for making things happen for you. Ultimately each one of us needs to understand what our actual requirement is, where we currently stand. How we are communicating while writing e-mails, or during the telephonic conversations and face to face discussions. What all changes we need to do so that we develop a strong personality. Think about it!

Accept people the way they are

The **toughest thing** is to accept others in the way they are. We invest our positive energy in others, but mostly we fail to receive back the response that we were expecting in return.

The reason we need to start accepting others as is because the expectation we create here weakens our own personality.

A short story to understand this:

A mother once gave a bicycle each to twin brothers and asked them not to touch each other's bicycles, taking care of the bicycle was their own responsibility.

Days passed and the mother noticed one brother had kept his bicycle so clean, parked it nicely to avoid any damage but the second brother was completely opposite, the bicycle was thrown on the ground and not parked, the tires were full of mud, dust and scratches were all that the mother could see on the bicycle.

One day the first brother asked his mother, *"why my brother never takes care of his belongings, he is so careless and carefree that whatever toys & things you provide to him always get broken first, and* ***ultimately I have to share mine with him*** *as I love my brother and cannot see him sad".*

The mother smiled & said very politely that "just ***for a second think of this bicycle as your life****, and we know that we solely are responsible for our own life. You may love to polish your life each day by learning, gaining knowledge and by facing challenges positively and the other may not be the same as you, may not be able to learn, gain knowledge or polish their life, their conduct & basic habits. It is always good to share, it is always good to help others, but only up to a certain limit.* ***When we start expecting from others that like us, they must also change for good, we end up losing focus on our own life.***

I am not saying that you should not share things with your brother or that your expectation from him to become like you is wrong, but the time has come when you must let him understand the importance of money, the importance of these things that he is getting so easily in his life.

You must share all those things that are in your capacity of sharing for example cake, chocolates, knowledge, your skills, your suggestions but when I am giving something individually to each one of you then ***let your brother learn the importance of those things by himself.***

You should accept him the way he is and ***must allow him to learn from his own mistakes.*** *It will be hard to say no to him, but once his bicycle will be completely broken and yours will remain new like today, he will surely understand his mistakes. When his bicycle will be broken or will be of no use, he must understand that the same bicycle his brother has is still functioning so well.*

Understand my child, it is not at all about the materials or the bicycle, these things come & go, but your conduct, habits & your representation will remain with you forever. Allow your brother to understand that he can be either careless & carefree and keep complicating things for himself, or he can also develop good habits & keep his toys and gifts clean and in good conditions."

The mother here tried to share some deep knowledge about life by taking an example of her son's bicycle.

But, mother, all that you just said to me is for my brother, but what should I do to help him to improve his habits of keeping things and becoming more sincere in his life?? the son asked another question.

Mother answered *"Just start accepting him the way he is and* ***do not judge him or consider him low or weak as compared to***

yourself. Also, do not go beyond your own boundaries to make his life so easy that he never is able to learn the importance of these things. *It is only a bicycle today; you can give yours and wait for your round to come. But if you think of your bicycle as your life, then for a while you stopped, your focus has deviated as you expected others to work and behave like you, and if the other person fails you get disappointed."*

This is just to be considered a fable that gives us clarity to understand the art of "acceptance". We must provide others with the opportunity to learn but on their own. A good personality, good conduct & behaviour is always noticed, and so many people learn from it. Do not give your own life, your own bicycle to them, but allow them to understand this with their own experience, you can surely be a good example for them, now it depends on if they really want to learn something from you or not.

This is just an imaginary story and let us not focus on the facts that how children so small can learn these intense things, rather look at the bicycle as your own life where we expect too much from other people, and many times their habits & conduct are not acceptable to us.

We sometimes go beyond our limits to see them change for their own good and this can really disappoint us if the other person does not really want to change!

This indirectly affects our own life; the **expectation is the biggest mistake we make every now & then.** We must accept the other person, do not worry or panic, the right time will come, and life has its own ways of telling people what is best for them.

How are we saving ourselves here and how it is linked to our presentation & personality?

The answer is very simple to understand; we greet the most annoying person happily and genuinely with an open heart. We show them our respect.

Our personality and conduct should be so strong & powerful that we are able to ignore the odd things we see around us, becoming a perfect example by working on our own communication skills, tone, AB quotient and our personality. **We allow them to silently learn from us without offending them at all.**

Even after this if the other person does not want to change, then accept them for what they are. Maybe there are still some more areas for us to build upon that can impact other people's way of thinking. So, let us keep on learning and lead by example.

Do what you say or commit!

A person who respects work ethics will never retract his/her statement or commitments seeing the benefits or disadvantages at any later stage. This is where we express & represent ourselves the most.

What really happens if we retract our commitment? Once you retract from the correct statement on seeing the benefits or disadvantages, then no matter how good your first impression and personality appeared to someone, **you will immediately lose that person's trust & confidence in you.**

The fulfilment of our commitments from time to time is self-explanatory for the cause when we are trying to portray a strong, powerful personality or if we genuinely have one!

Never over-commit for the things that are beyond your authority or abilities. Now you know how to say "no" or how to show your disagreement. You have learnt how to put the most crucial point forward for saving yourself from any false commitment.

Once you commit something, no matter how much effort you need to put for it, stick to your words & finish it.

English speaking! A challenge?

English is a commonly spoken language, and this last section talks about the fear so many people have while interacting with clients or stakeholders in English.

Most people know and understand the English language as per their daily interactions. The only challenge that we have is to confidently interact with someone in the English language. Below are some quick tips you can follow to enhance your communication skills to speak in a confident and polite tone.

No one is going to judge you if you are not very fluent in English communication like others, try these techniques and see wonderful changes in yourself:

- Start watching Hollywood movies, make a habit of watching one English movie with **pronunciation of these words**. We are not going to focus on the accent here, but we are trying to get habitual with words, phrases and commonly used sentences. Try to focus on the **pronunciation of these words**. I rarely recommend someone to start with news headlines or by reading a newspaper article which is generally the case, but to some, it can be boring or not the area of interest! **In my view, learning becomes easy only when we enjoy it.** So, pick any genre of movie that you like, but do watch 1 English movie a week and do this for 3-4 months without a miss. If you are a beginner then initially it may appear a little annoying to you, but gradually your ears & mind will start grasping new words, its pronunciation and a couple of good sentences that you usually hear at your workplace.

- Listening to English music tracks is another best way to make yourself habitual to interact fluently in English. I remember those initial days when we were in the last year of college, and I used to listen to English songs by keeping the lyrics in front of me as I followed the track by singing it along. After 4-5 attempts at one song, I was able to sing the same by clearly pronouncing the words. Voice & pitch obviously should be avoided as our focus is on getting habitual to English sentences and words that are to be pronounced loudly. I was happy murmuring the English songs daily. This has really helped me to work upon my confidence and verbal communication.

- Do not restrict yourself while using the English language as a medium to interact with someone. It should not matter to us as to how many grammatical errors we make when we attempt to speak in English as this can be gradually learnt with practice. English is a commonly used language worldwide; you **must get rid of any kind of fear** that you can be judged by people and what these people will think! Only Practise and practise can make you perfect. If you already are very good and fluent in verbally spoken English then help others to develop this skill by accepting minor errors or grammatical mistakes you hear from them. And if you still need to work on verbal English communication, then try these techniques and you yourself will be amazed by the results.

- If you have a lot of abroad client interactions & are hesitant because of verbal English and need more specific training or guidance, then just do as I told! Spend some time with yourself, understand your requirements, do some research about the latest communication techniques and tips, & go for the best training that matches your expectations. **There is no age limit to learn and polish your skills.**

Success Principle 8

Smart work Vs Hard work Rule

Time to introspect again! Answer these questions and be very honest to yourself, as you know, nobody is judging you at all.

Q1. Is it right to say that smart work always wins over Hard work, Yes or no?

Ans. _______________

Q2. Currently, how do you see yourself, as a smart worker or as a hard worker?

Ans. _______________

Q3. Recall any 2 scenarios where you had worked smartly to get the result & were able to avoid hard work! (Spend only 2-3 mins on this)

Ans. ______________________________________

Q4. What do you think, to what extent the result can vary for Smart work vs Hard work?

Ans. ______________________________________

Let us find out the truth about hard work & smart work now and find the answers to all such questions.

Do not separate Hard work from Smart work

You all know these famous personalities who achieved enormous success and fame in life but only based on hard work, surely, they **did it very smartly.**

- Famous former professional American basketball player Michael Jordan's

  His desire to get better each day with his hard work made him a champion. As per many reports, he spent the entire summer doing two practice sessions in one single day and that too for six days a week, shooting at least 500 jump shots in each practice. That is more than 6,000 practice shots each week!

"I've always believed that if you put in the work, the results will come. I do not do things half-heartedly. Because I know if I do, then I can expect half-hearted results."

- Michael Jordan

- Indian Prime Minister Shri Narendra Modi

At the age of 70, he follows a strict routine by getting up at 5:00 am in the morning, does yoga & meditation daily no matter in which country or place he is in. He spends his whole day as a hard-working leader starting from attending the meetings with ministers, attending important calls, an inspection of the work etc. At this age also, he has such an amazing zeal & so much passion for work that even after coming back home, he prefers to complete his pending task before going to bed. His love for his country, his dedication & hard work is remarkable.

कड़ी मेहनत कभी थकान नहीं लाती वह संतोष लाती हैं

English translation:

"Hard Work never brings fatigue. It brings satisfaction."

- Narendra Modi

- Tim Cook, Chief Executive Officer of Apple, is amongst the most hard-working successful people of the world. According to USA Today, he usually wakes at 3:45 a.m. and described himself as a "fitness nut" in a Fortune interview and has a morning routine like those of many other successful leaders. He is known for his workaholic & hard-working attitude as he is the first person to reach the office & the last one to leave it! Does this not include hard work?

"It's hard to edit. It's hard to stay focused. And yet, we know we'll only do our best work if we stay focused. And so, you know, the hardest decisions we made are all the things not to work on, frankly."

- Tim Cook

- Mark Cuban is an American entrepreneur, television personality, media proprietor, and an investor who has achieved renowned success by hard work done so smartly. In one of his blogs, he mentioned about starting his first company, he routinely stayed up until two in the morning reading about new software and did not take any vacation for seven years.

Can you possibly imagine a person who did not take a vacation for seven long years?

Be it Narendra Modi, Mark Cuban, Jordan, or Tim Cook, just think for a while, was it possible for them to be so successful in life without doing hard work and without going beyond their normal limits, without finding their highest potential?

With the above-mentioned examples, I just wanted you to understand that **you can NEVER separate HARD WORK FROM SUCCESS.** These famous personalities have worked too hard to get to this successful position. So, the **"Smartly done Hard Work" i**s something we all need to do, that will reward us with unlimited opportunities & growth at the workplace and in personal life!

Change of approach is surely required, rather than doing **Harder Hard Work** start doing ***Smarter Hard work!*** You cannot just run from the hard work; the result will be as slow as you can imagine if you really are trying to avoid hard work and finding shortcuts for completing even the smallest assignment!

Now shifting the spotlight back to the famous personalities, how smarter hard work would have worked for them, it is easy to understand. Even when they all worked so hard, they were able to complete all of their planned tasks. They are strict about following a well-planned schedule that includes Yoga, meditation, healthy diet, focus on fitness, developed a strong, bold personality at the personal front and at the workplace as they are the most committed persons.

Never forget that hard work was, is and will always be the base for success & growth in life. So, there **can never be a comparison between smart work & hard work.** Picking up this title "Smart work" VS "Hard Work" was simply a trick to see if you really differentiate between smart & hard work.

Now we clearly understand that **smart work is an extended version of hard work to get maximum productivity and best results within a shorter time frame.**

It is not as easy as you think, not even for the king of the jungle!

The Lion, as for food, needs to always run after his prey by maintaining a specific speed for some time to catch him. If only smart work would have been sufficient alone to achieve the goal then a lion, who is the king of the jungle, would just apply all types of smart techniques to lure his prey near him without running after him. But is it possible? Of course not!

Time to apply this principle of doing **Smarter Hard Work** to get extraordinary rewards. If even for a second you have any self-doubts or feel that *"I am reading this book which talks about so many amazing things, but I am different, or I am not lucky enough to create such wonderful life-changing experiences"*, then I will remind you again that this power and the courage to bring a change is present within you, you just need to dig deeper to tap into its potential. If Tim Cook, Narendra Modi, Jordan & so many others can do it, then **you can do it too!**

Do you think that they were famous from the very beginning of their careers? They all became famous after they did something extraordinary in their life. Everybody talks about this new Normal, I personally feel, and I think you would also agree that there is nothing "NORMAL" about this new normal.

Market competition will increase more & more as clients are

looking only for the organisations that can provide them 24*7 service from a remote location. As this pandemic has shaken sustainability all over the world, every client who wants a service is looking for reliable organisations with capable leaders & resources that can go beyond their limits and can work hard to make projects/processes successful for them. In this new normal we are already into a phase where we are preparing ourselves, just in case if history repeats itself anytime in future. Fingers crossed that we never ever see a situation like this again, but this cannot stop us from thinking out of the box, from preparing ourselves for anything that can break off our growth rate ever again.

As an associate, you need to really outshine with your skills, behaviour, attitude and learning to match up the trends & market demands that are changing every now & then. For this, you need to work upon your existing work techniques.

There is always a scope of improvement in everything we do in our lives, i.e., always try to get to a new version of yours. Every single element we are discussing or have already discussed is just like digging deep into the ground to get to the success & abundance. Remember **the "Rule of 24 meters down in 24 hours!"??** The universe has never reflected favouritism as these 24 hours are given equally to all of us. It is now upon you as to how much smarter hard work you do so that fame, success, money, and happiness themselves start following you! This cannot happen without taking efforts.

Let me share one more live example here, this person may not be very famous as of now but is regularly working on upgrading the existing version to a new one as there is always scope for it. This person works honestly & with full commitment to the organisation from Monday to Saturday. It does not really bother her if she needs to work on weekends for some critical work submissions. She is a self-motivated person who strongly believes in "change" and the power of positive thinking that exists in the universe.

Married in 2019, she never had tried to run from her personal responsibilities at home. This person loves to take some time out on weekends to learn something new. She focuses on her health & fitness, along with the work she does. She spends her weekend only to polish her skills & always keeps herself busy with her hobbies & passion that makes her happy.

She is a student from science stream and amongst the top performers at her school & in her college. She had to leave B.Sc. (Hons) as the college principal asked her to leave the college because she had some critical health issues and she fainted 2-3 times during her lectures. The principal of the college being the decision-maker asked her to leave the college as it was creating a lot of disturbance for other students. After 2 years of complete bed rest, she somehow managed to complete her graduation. She also added a couple of management diplomas to her academic's qualification in the next few years. For her post-graduation, when she planned to appear for the exams, her health ditched her once again. As she got hospitalised again due to prevailing health concerns, she had to leave her studies in between & was bedridden for a year again. She always wanted to go beyond her limits; her optimistic approach was so good that after 1 year, she completed her post-graduation along with her job, irrespective of her health conditions.

During the initial years of her career, she met with an accident and got a major backbone injury and her pre-existing health concerns still prevailed. She was unable to walk or even sit properly. She had severe migraine concerns, anxiety, blood cells disorder, cysts, knee and backbone injury, hypersensitive lungs suffocation concern and what not? But she never used her health as an excuse for not working hard. She still cannot do certain exercises, weightlifting, running, or too much forward bending because of this permanent backbone injury she suffered from in the past.

Her interest in writing poems, articles and quotations developed right after she lost her father at the age of 13. A time came when because of repeated failures and struggles, she went into a deep depression and became hopeless towards her life. All her positive energies vanished, and she was not able to take it anymore and she attempted an almost successful suicide during her teenage.

Somehow, she managed to bring herself back from this severe depression by getting support from her mother & her best friend (her husband). She started following Nichiren Buddhism and did whatever it takes to understand the purpose of her life. The knowledge she gained through Buddhism philosophy changed her life as there was no looking back in her life thereafter.

Her passion & hobby today is to encourage others through her own life experiences so that no one else tries to end their life like her, which she regrets each day.

She understood this with the help of mediation, Buddhism & self-introspection that **not all are lucky to get a second chance just like her.** This is the only life and the only chance we get to do something extraordinary, to go beyond our limitations, to encourage others so that they do not miss their chance of doing something extraordinary.

This lady is none other than the author of this book! So, after my 9-10 hours of office shift, and after completing the household activities, whatever time I get, I am putting in 1000% efforts to write this book.

I always loved writing poems, blogs, articles, and this idea of becoming an author came to my mind when I tested COVID-19 positive with a bad lung infection and was in isolation for 21 days. This was the best time that I dug deep into myself to find the extraordinary me.

So, this is how **I took COVID-19 as an opportunity and chance to explore the higher levels of my potential**. Trust me, every result that you expect to be extraordinary demands real hard work and I was all ready for that, I am utilising my weekends & after office hours to complete this book for those who believe in me & for those whom I believe in, my family, friends & of course my readers.

We must cut down all our distractions, for achieving something extraordinary in our life. My first step towards it was not to check any of my social media accounts as they are the major reason for our distractions. I can assure **you that you gain 50 times better focus on whatever work you do if you are able to work upon these distractions.**

So, it is the same Shivali Tandon having all those health issues as it is. My backbone injury doesn't allow me to do prolonged sitting, but that's ok, I had to train my mind to cut down all negative thoughts and replace them with positive ones. I know that God has given strength to each one of us to fight various challenges & we just need to tap into that passion, strength, and determination again & again until we are victorious.

This book writing may not be a very big deal for some people out there, maybe just a good thing for some others, or maybe appreciable by a few more **but for me,** it's part of those small steps I take every day so that I can become a little better "me" than yesterday, just like many hard-working famous personalities we just read about.

Trying not to deviate you from the "hard work done smartly" principle but if I, as an author is taking this huge responsibility to bring about a difference into your life through these principles, then I must assure you that these principles are tried & tested on my own life and are very effective **if applied with complete sincerity & planning.**

Our shift from Hard work to Smarter hard work will surely require some specific smart working techniques and now is the time to follow these smart working techniques.

Proactive Approach: 8A

The Smart techniques for doing smarter Hard work:

If possible, please try to read below flowchart at least 2 times to deeply transform yourself into a smarter hard worker. These smarter hard-working techniques can be applied both at the workplace as well in your personal life. You can also refer to this flow chart anytime anywhere when you are stuck somewhere due to multiple tasks that are on your plate.

Smart at Planning

⇩

Smart at Research

⇩

Smart at Analysing

⇩

Smart at ETA

⇩

Smart with Distractions

⇩

Smart at real-time feedback & testing

⇩

Smart at delivering the final work

Let us see how this Proactive Approach works:

1. Smart at Planning

After completing any task first use the P-L-A-N Rule (No

Stress, High-performance voyage from Proactive Approach: 2A) where we learnt how to plan, learn, apply, and navigate our actions. Set priorities to monitor your progress for each assigned task.

2. Smart at Research

Once you have planned on how to execute these tasks, do not be in a hurry to just start it. It is better to do some research about the work you need to accomplish by referring to any existing report, or a document that uses the same format. For new creative ideas, it is better to do online research by going through some basics about the work.

3. Smart at Analysing

Now when you did research on the task assigned to you, even if you were able to learn everything there was to learn about the topic, you must be having 1 or 2 questions in your mind as every company has a different way of working. It would be great if you can quickly check with your manager regarding the purpose of the task, or what we are trying to achieve here. Always be smart to analyse your manager's working style & how he works and take guidance from him. Even the smallest suggestion from a leader or manager can improve the result.

4. Smart at ETA

ETA is a term used to measure the expected time of completion of any work.

Setting up the correct ETA keeps you awake and active as

you always have a deadline to submit your work. Ascertain your working speed and potential, and never overcommit to your manager or employer. If you need 2 hours to complete your work, convey your ETA as 3 hours, always keep a buffer whenever it is possible. Submit your task as soon as you complete it but keeping an ETA buffer helps you get a good quality of work.

5. Smart with Distractions

Initially, when you started your work for the day, you were full of energy, but gradually distractions have increased as people around you are taking breaks in between the work. You are trying to focus on your work and trying to implement new creative ideas, but somehow you are not progressing at the pace that you planned you would. Nothing is going as per the planned schedule, and this is the Distraction that will not allow you to perform at your best. So, it is time to take a break of 10-15 minutes, get some fresh air, have a cup of coffee, talk to a friend, or do whatever you like, to instantly recharge yourself. For better creative ideas & productivity, take this short 10 minutes break after every 2 hours, but make sure those 2 hours are fully productive.

6. Smart at real-time feedback & testing

Be it coding, testing, designing, or preparing an excel report, for any work we do, it is very important to not let our efforts go in vain. This can happen when we avoid/miss to collect real-time feedback on our work from someone within our team or from the one who assigned us the task. We make the hard work **harder** by not sharing and discussing the real-time progress of the work we do. A smart worker always knows how to save his time & get the nearly perfect result that is expected out of his work.

If you are not in the right direction, this real-time feedback will save your time and with suggestions, you can make changes during the initial level of your work, instead of sending the bulk of reports and data after doing a lot of hard work & then getting a negative response from the manager or the 2nd party only to start from scratch again. There is no harm in doing experiments during work, as a little creativity will not hurt anybody, but those should be tested and checked in between. Collecting real-time feedback for your work will make your work better in quality and quantity both.

7. Smart at delivering the final work

Being Smart at delivering the work is nothing but to always have a Plan B and Plan C ready with us. Sometimes even after getting clear expectations from the client or the employer, we fail to deliver the result, which is up to their expectations, not because there was any mistake on our part but because of differences in the way the idea was implemented, one person may like it and the other may not.

To solve this problem, a smart worker will always have some details ready with him as PATH B and PATH C, it would only require him to make little changes in the existing work, i.e. PATH A, and with less effort, he can present PATH B or C to the client or employer and they now get the option to choose from all three paths.

Just for an example, a designer prepared a Brand Logo Design, and he did not restrict his creativity only to one design, he made slight changes in the artwork of each of the three logos so that if the best one gets rejected, he has 2 more options to present. Now the catch here is you should **never reveal all the paths in one go** to the client or employer, these Path B and Path C are only to be presented if your best work gets rejected at any stage.

Use your wisdom and enjoy doing Hard work but SMARTLY!

Smartly Done Hard - Work

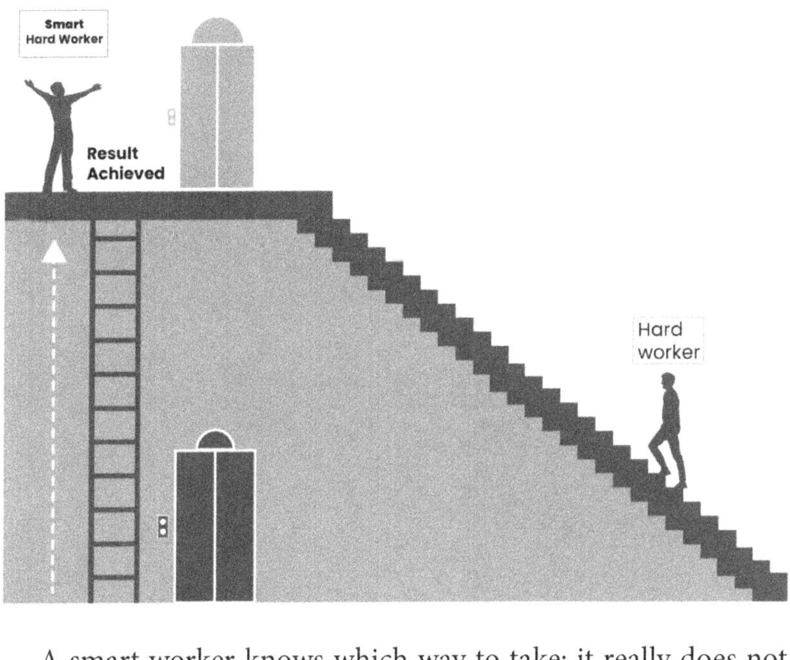

A smart worker knows which way to take; it really does not matter which path you chose, a normal staircase, shortcut by ladder or to use a lift, the result will be the achieved in both the cases, **but the impact will be different.** If you follow these 5 smart techniques sincerely every time when you get a task assigned, you can achieve an **extraordinary result** which is different from a standard/normal result. A hard-working person will also get to a nearly matching result, but a **Smart Hard worker will surely come up with something extraordinary and creative in shorter period of time.**

Success Principle 9

Mantras that work wonders!

Do not consider these mantras as spells or Gyan (knowledge) given by me to you!

I am neither a guru nor a teacher, so I cannot give you these Mantras to follow! But at the same time, I feel that these three Guru Mantras should be part of your life. The truth is that only "you" can add or remove these principles from your life!

Merge these three Mantras in your life to see the exponential transformation in yourself & in your surroundings.

"Time", "Universe" and "God" are our first Gurus or mentors of life. If we align our life with these three guides, then surely, we will be able to achieve extraordinary success and happiness in life.

As whatever we do & whatever we get is instilled and circulated in the universe with God's blessing.

It is like "cause & effect phenomena" and I understood this phenomenon after joining Nichiren Buddhism. "Cause & Effect" is a universal law and can be noticed in various other philosophies which talk about Life & Karma.

Cause & Effect phenomena
Proactive Approach: 9A

Cause & Effect phenomena in simple terms mean, whatever we give to the universe we get it back in a certain way. Maybe the appearance can be different, but this is how the universe balances itself **by accepting whatever we give to it and throwing it back with the same intensity towards us.**

That is why I have a strong belief in the "power of positive thinking" and the thoughts we have in our mind. In whatever way we transmit our energies towards the universe, it always responds back to us with the same intensity.

Why are we discussing this here? You must be confused about finding a connection between performing with your highest potential and this "cause & effect phenomena".

You must know that the most influential and powerful people of the world are the people who never forgot their moral values & their past struggle from where they started their journey to reach this successful point.

These people always remained grounded, believed in cause & effect philosophy, respected everyone, and tried to always add value to whatever they do so that it makes a difference in other's lives too. **This is the purest form of success one can achieve** by being down to earth, courageous, and hard-working. They became powerful and rich, yet always went beyond their limits to help others.

First Mantra:
Find a Mentor or a Guide for Life!

We now know that we always have 3 mystical mentors in our life, the "Time" that teaches us the value of life, the "God" that guides us and the "Universe" that responds to us as per our thought process.

Apart from these mystical elements, reasonably so many of us are still alone in the crowd. We are surrounded by so many friends, family, colleagues, relatives, yet alone emotionally & mentally.

If you have already found that person who can always guide you correctly, then you are blessed and you need to take a lot of guidance from this person. A mentor or a guide is the one who is committed to his/her own life principles or moral values; this person always does what he/she says & follows the path of correct deeds.

You cannot make that person your mentor or guide who is already living his/her life on lies, maintaining a fake personality, and helping others only for personal interest. He might act noble by sharing his ideas & suggestions, but you somehow doubt that he himself misses following these principles he always talks about.

There are thousands of people around you, but this **mentor is like a Moon in the sky and as a precious pearl in the sea.**

A mentor is the one who has always inspired me, who has always guided me to achieve the best.

How would you be able to understand if this person can become your mentor?

You can understand this by finding a "relation" and "connection" between this person at a mystical level, i.e. this person's aura will reflect so much optimistic vibes that your heart & mind will automatically start building a connection with this person. The AB quotient & L-N-E approach plays a major role to build this connection if you are genuinely ready to learn from this person by having an open-minded, positive AB quotient.

Sometimes **we just have to feel the cosmic energies around us** without doing a lot of calculations about what & how, i.e. the time you will notice this person who really inspires you, your heart will automatically send strong signals to your mind that "I want to be like him" or "I want to learn from him", or "I want to absorb as much knowledge as I can from this person" to change for the better.

This will be the moment of joy when your mind will tell you that you have got "HOPE", as you found someone special who can be your guide, mentor, or a teacher for life. It is the same situation when a man who is drowning clutches at a straw to save himself from sinking deep inside the darkness. This person who inspires us will become the straw that will surely pull us out of any kind of darkness for which we need to keep trying. Keep holding the straw no matter what!

Why to have this one special mentor in our life?

Because human beings are a bucket full of emotions & thoughts. We, humans, tend to easily get influenced by good or bad and that is normal to happen but keeping yourself around this positive & extraordinary personality always influences your life for the better each day. Sometimes you know a person who has this astounding persona & you literally are a fan of this person but have never expressed this. You may find him/her as an idol person to follow in terms of behaviour, success, habits, conduct & finances etc.

Now, close your eyes for just 2mins, think of such a person, no matter how far or close they are, no matter what religion they follow. Just think of this person who has done some great inspiring things in life, maybe these things may not appear so great to others, but for you, those things have left a deep meaning & impact on your life.

The **purpose** is simple, if a log of fire does not ignite easily with a single matchstick then we either use more than 1 matchstick to burn it or we simply put an already burning wooden log to the whole stack of wood so that it gets more heat & catches fire.

The same is the condition of human beings. At the workplace, we are surrounded by different types of people; one person out of this crowd can be so powerful and positive that he/she can ignite your passion for success. Some out of this crowd can be dominating and may always talk negatively that you end up absorbing their negative vibes.

It is very important to stay around people who are positive & are working extraordinarily hard, and your heart keeps telling you that you should follow this person's footsteps.

Direct Guidance opportunity:

So, if you notice someone in your surroundings and your heart tells you that *"this one person has to be followed as he inspires me a lot, this one person can guide me better, even if he criticises me, I will be able to accept it as this will be for my own good"*. When you have this kind of acceptance for someone in your surrounding, then consider him as your **Direct Guide or teacher.**

Proactive Approach: 9B

Action required by you whenever you find this direct guide or mentor in your surroundings:

- Instead of wasting time scrolling up and down on social media and looking at what others are doing in their life, sit with this one person who inspires you. Tell him you love his/her work ethics, management skills, time management skills, his/her AB quotients or whatever you like about him.
- First, build the trust and then share with this person your struggles with an open heart. Let the person know about your goals & where do you see yourself after a few years?
- If the person is extraordinary, just like the moon in the sky and if your heart has signalled it correctly, then there must be some life-changing struggles this person had faced in his life too. Allow him to share that with you. We are not going to call him a mentor or teacher on his face, but that is a bond you need to create with him sooner or later. This person can be anywhere at your workplace, home, or in your friend circle.

The time you take even a single action based upon this person's experience or guidance, that would be a very valuable moment and will be your first step towards becoming extraordinary.

Do not restrict yourself while talking to this person or to learn from his experiences. You never know when & how **you may get**

so charged & encouraged that you might start leading by self-experienced examples for others around you.

Did I mention anywhere that this guide or a mentor whom you secretly admire can only be 1 individual person in your life?

Sometimes it is rare to get even one such person around us who is genuinely extraordinary in his own life and in his own actions, but if you have more than one, you are extremely blessed.

Utilise your time by talking to such people. They can be that **burning log of wood** to ignite the growth in your career path!

Now there is no need for me to tell my readers what should be asked, what should be discussed and how you should discuss your challenges with this mentor for life. It completely depends upon your AB quotient, your strong determination towards L-N-E principle, your presentation & personality. On noticing all this, these extraordinary people will surely come forward to guide you. They will distinguish you from the crowd and will place the spotlight directly on you!

Always remember,

"A mentor in your life will always tell you to do things right but will never force you to do "Extraordinary" things rightly & smartly; extraordinary achievements can only be experienced after a lot of hard work & determination. This is how you will reveal your own success secrets in future with someone who has an "extraordinary hunger" for learning & acceptance."

- Shivali Tandon

Your work potential will increase just by having a good honest mentor around you! Focus on GOOD & HONEST - **GOOD** means; this mentor helps you in finding the solution to your problem & never gives up, **HONEST** because only he can pinpoint your weaknesses, and can highlight those areas where you need to improve!

If you are working somewhere no matter what industry it is - manufacturing, IT, Financial market etc., someone is always there in your surroundings to whom you can look up to as a mentor or a guide. This mentor can be someone who has hired you or someone who is always full of energy & is optimistic.

Indirect Guidance opportunities:

So, this section is one of my favourites and **I spend 80% of my free time** with these Indirect Mentors. **Indirect mentors are very easy to find but are very tough to be followed!**

Let me tell you very honestly that in real life, I only have 1-2 extraordinary people who inspire me with their actions & deeds, and I have learnt a lot from them. They are and always will be my prime guide & critics who can pinpoint the worst in me.

Apart from this, whatever extraordinary goal I am trying to achieve in my life and whatever transformation I was able to bring into my life is **because of this indirect guidance.**

Indirect guidance means following some very successful & acknowledged hard-working people with the help of media and technology, where with one click, you can listen to their guidance anytime, anywhere! However, we are unable to get direct guidance from these mentors in a one-to-one meeting, but if we try to find the answers sincerely then from one way or the other, we could get unlimited answers and possibilities to start this transformation of our life.

The secret to indirect guidance is that the mentor cannot meet you but can give you unlimited inspirational ideas. Now it is completely up to us to either ignore these indirect suggestions or to really try to implement the same to create our own successful experiences.

Here are a couple of mentors I follow with all my sincerity & dedication. I just love to hear their guidance and to implement their suggestive techniques on a day-to-day basis.

List of my extraordinary Mentors starts here:

1. **Dr. Daiskau Ikeda,** who is a Japanese Buddhist philosopher, an educator, author, and nuclear disarmament advocate. He has served as the third president and then honorary president of the Soka Gakkai.

2. **Shri Sadhguru,** whose actual name is Jaggi Vasudev and he is helping people to change their lives for better as a Yogi himself. He is the founder & the guide of Isha Foundation, that is a non-profit spiritual organisation.

3. **Dr. Vivek Bindra,** who is an Entrepreneur, Motivational Speaker, CEO Coach, and his amazing journey from a Monk to a successful leader/coach, is so inspiring. He is spreading happiness in millions of lives through his work.

4. **Anthony Jay Robbins** is famous with his name "Tony Robbins' an American author, coach, motivational speaker, and philanthropist. This person's positive influence can easily be sensed through his books and videos. He will guide you to

awaken the Giant within you.

5. **Oprah Winfrey** is an American talk show host, television producer, actress, author, and philanthropist and what not! Her struggles are not hidden from the world and she inspires many of us with her own life experiences.

So even if you do not have such a guide yet, then find one for yourself! Open the internet browser or YouTube and just read about these extraordinary personalities. You can also go through their videos, lectures, or books, in whatever way **you want to reach out to them indirectly**. Also, you must note that these are the personalities that had left a major impact on my life & influenced me when I compared my own struggles of life to them, but it does not mean that only these five can be your indirect mentors. You must find them by yourself, as I already told you your eyes would see them, and your heart will signal your mind at their presence in your life. You **must find your moon in the sky & a precious pearl in the ocean by yourself.**

For this, we need to get rid of those distractions that I mentioned earlier. Let us not waste a single minute looking at the lives of others on social media, by uselessly checking unproductive videos or messages. Rather try to take guidance from these indirect mentors that can enlighten your mind with their life-changing experiences and suggestions.

This habit of watching 1 or 2 videos from any of the indirect mentors can totally change your approach towards life. I have immense gratitude for having met them through their videos and books. I really feel blessed that I was able to connect with them so quickly.

So, did you not find your indirect mentor (s)? If not, then it is time to seek the one now.

Second Mantra: SILENCE is your weapon in need!

At the workplace & in personal life, we sometimes meet people who drain out our positive energies. This happens so fast that we do not even realise how much loss we have faced due to this.

We had learnt about how to put our point forward correctly, about our tone, communication skills during normal discussions to aggressive one's. During these arguments, we get offended so easily that we literally use harsh tones or may show others our aggressive side.

Silence as a weapon can fix the issues or can become the reason for destruction as time passes by. So when I say silence is your weapon **in need,** I clearly mean that we must use this weapon **at the correct time & place only.**

The last "Angry" speaker always loses the battle!

Your workplace is no different than your family, but yes, it is just like your second family or home where you spend the most productive hours of the day. Like 2 sisters or 2 brothers fighting at home, not all the time, but sometimes that intense fight can occur at your workplace too. There can be multiple reasons for a fight at the office and here, our focus is not to look at the reasons.

Our focus should be upon how to **put our opinions forward with dignity & respect**! Just to clarify, the fight we are talking about here is a verbal argument only.

A heated argument that may have started due to new process implementation and your disagreement on that decision, followed by detesting towards the person, or even for not getting help from this person in the past. There can be any reason when any heated argument converts itself into an actual verbal fight.

Anger being the enemy of every single person on this earth works as fuel in the fire. No matter how much we meditated this morning, how calm we were a moment ago, at this moment **this anger is so powerful that it has erased all good memories from our mind!!**

If your anger is spoiling your life, then look for some good anger management techniques. Meditation, chanting of mantras and 7 chakras balancing techniques has helped so many of us to overcome anger & stress to a great extent.

But during a heated argument between you and your colleague, or manager or with anyone else in the office, if the tone of your voice is very harsh, then you have already lost the battle!

Sometimes the topic of the argument gets diluted in between, **due to the way we talk to each other.** Always try to stay at **LEVEL-B** of "The Three Levels Voice Tone Model 6A" where we confidently, diplomatically yet softly put our points forward while maintaining our tone as moderately polite as we can.

When during such heated arguments where you and your colleagues are losing control of your temper, try to put your point only once or twice. Or in case the other person is not able to understand the same, then take a step back and take a deep breath… pause for 5,4,3,2,1 seconds… and pull yourself back immediately out of the argument and it's time to use the weapon, i.e. your **"SILENCE"**.

Believe me that with this you have already won half of the battle. Your silence does not mean that you have agreed to the other person's point or that you are running away from the argument, it simply means giving yourself & the other person ample time to recall what just had happened.

At a psychological level, your mind appreciates you that you were not the person who crossed the limit, which is part of basic workplace ethics. Your tone was not harsh; you tried to put your point forward with all decency; still, the other person kept on fighting or was using a harsh tone.

So, now comes the third party here who acts as **a conflict management team**, because I am an HR, I know this very well that no matter how big the issue or concern maybe, but no one can go against the code of conduct of the company.

Harsh decisions are taken against those associates who usually lost their temper & reacted in an unethical way towards the other party. In some cases, they might even be asked to leave the organisation. Ultimately for any company, their culture & associate's AB quotient matters the most.

Logically when the conflict management team sits with these 2 people who had a heated argument, they first focus on how you reacted instead of what you reacted to. The good part about having a conflict management team is that you get a chance to put your point forward. Half the battle you had already won & rest of it you have to win now!

It is up to the effectiveness of your communication & logical reasonings behind agreeing or disagreeing to the actual reason for the argument. If your point is valid and makes some sense, then management will surely re-consider it. But in a case where you argued for a wrong point then also your "SILENCE" (that you used earlier) will save you from any harsh decision to be made against you because you tried to put your point decently. The same would be confirmed by the witnesses who saw the whole situation.

Also, a very important thing which happens if you choose to be SILENT during a heated argument is that you give the other person a moment to introspect his opinion and behaviour. With this weapon of SILENCE, you always have the upper hand as you never reveal your intentions & thoughts to the other person, kept yourself calm and now who is in stress? Do not worry you will anyhow get an opportunity to keep your point again in front of concerned decision-makers, i.e. the management, just do not lose your temper as it is the devil during any heated argument or fight. **Do not give management a single reason to doubt your AB quotient.**

The other person will get confused and would be in a dilemma whether he was arguing for a valid point or not.

Lastly, a few other benefits of using this wonderful weapon "the Silence" are:

- Firstly, you are always showing respect towards the set code of conduct of the organisation and the company in return always appreciate this sensibility of yours.
- Secondly, you can save all your energies. This energy of anger that you trapped in the prison of silence can later be utilised to recall what the other person said to you during the discussion

or argument; you now understand this person's point. You can now prepare your notes again and when the correct time comes, you are all set to put your point forward with valid reasons & logics this time. The one who had lost his temper had failed to hide his strategies and the reason for the argument. Now you already know the reasons due to which your opinion might get rejected and can rework on the disagreeable point.

Third Mantra:
Be aware of what's NOT HAPPENING rather notice what has happened already

We keep our ears open to stay alert & be aware of what is happening in our surroundings & in our life.

It is said that staying alert of things that are happening around make us powerful, out of many reasons a couple of them I would like to highlight here:

- Nobody can lie to you if you notice things very carefully.
- Nobody can compete with the level of confidence you carry as you know what was discussed, said & done during meetings, or during working hours and in general also at your home.
- The most alert people tend to grasp things quickly & easily, and with this, your L-N-E mode is active most of the time.
- You never miss the timelines for the assigned work; you never miss on the commitments done with others; you always stay away from "confusion".
- There are fewer chances of getting entangled into any conflictive argument & discussion as you are pretty alert & have most of

the details ready in your mind.

In this section, I would like you & all the other alert people to focus on **what is not happening in your life & in your surroundings.** I know it sounds strange that how can anybody notice something that is actually "not happening" at all. Alright! For understanding this, I request you to give a thought to each statement mentioned below, no pen or paper needed for this activity. You can simply check upon the first thought that comes to your mind:

Mr. A vs Mr. J

- **Mr. A** is very alert and aware of what is happening in his surroundings. His kind of alertness is such that he even wants to know what in general is happening in the office other than what he sees himself in his surroundings. Anybody who would like to get the news about what is happening comes to Mr. A, and asks him about it. So, you got me right, this type of alertness of Mr. A, for noticing things like - who got engaged, who got promoted, even the Human Resources team members are sometimes shocked when he shares, not very accurate, but nearly matching the hike percentage of people in the organisation. That means he has some rapport in the office & people share things with him, even the confidential information that must never be shared with anyone in the office just like the hike they are getting. He can tell anybody anytime that who married whom, who got the latest certification done, who attended the workshop sponsored by the company, who attended the training & how many training-hours benefit was given to a person. All of this out of jealousy may be or just out of curiosity.

- **Mr. J** is very alert, but his way of noticing things in the surroundings is different and opposite than that of **Mr. A.** He notices the happening in his surroundings, mostly for his own benefits. However, he is good at learning & is always aware, which client visited on which day, what were the client's major focus & concern areas, any latest training that happened in the organisation surely, he is aware of it, also about who all got the promotions and what updates are done on the company's website. He even remembers the smallest thing that happened in the cafeteria. For example, who all ate samosas (snacks) and who paid the bills today and yesterday and the day before yesterday, he can tell his team members about their pending payments confidently. So, as you can see, he is very clear about noticing & remembering things!

Who would you like to become Mr. A, or Mr. J? Please answer!

Ans. __________

The irony is, I do not want to be either like, **Mr. A,** or like **Mr. J.**

How about becoming like **Mr P.** who is focussed, aware, attentive about what is happening in the surrounding but in reality, he is more attentive about **"what's not happening in his surrounding".**

Let us understand Mr. P's way of noticing things with real-time scenarios:

1st scenario:

A very important training was conducted in the organisation but only for some specific members as decided by the management and as per project requirement. Now Mr. P did notice this, but his focus was on the point that such training would be beneficial for him as well, so why should he not be given a chance to get this training with others. Hope you got it now! He noticed something and **is aware of what he might be missing on** rather than focusing on what is happening with others; **this is a real hunger for success & growth.**

He went to the manager requesting for this training, what do you think the management would have decided?

Maybe they agreed, even if they rejected his request, he knows that he needs to do it by himself if it will add to his skills & learning.

2nd scenario:

The company asked so many of its associates to resign from their position as due to the pandemic of Covid-19 it was part of a business contingency plan. Out of 5 team members, 3 were asked to leave, but Mr. P and one of his colleagues remained with the organisation. Mr. P did notice that 3 members lost their jobs, he was surely concerned for them, **but** at the same time he was aware & he noticed that this did not happen with him**, the purpose of noticing the "unhappened event" always gives us an opportunity to find the best & the worst out of it.** So, Mr. P introspected, concluded his way of working is good and he may need to keep polishing his skills & working style so that his employment is always secured no matter how many pandemics show up. He was thankful for it. Just by changing the approach of thinking, how beautifully we can motivate ourselves. **The sense of responsibility towards his career stability & the organisation can clearly be sensed here.**

3rd scenario:

Do you remember **Mr. Rajat** from the earlier section, i.e., Success Principle 7: "The presentation of Me", who is a highly-skilled designer at the organisation and client wanted this designer to visit them personally at the client location for working individually on some new designs. Everybody knew about this and yet he was not selected for this amazing growth opportunity because he needs to become competent in his communications & his presentation skills. He hardly speaks English, and he would not have been able to understand the client's requirement. Yes, the company would have sent one translator with him for getting the work done, but that is not the correct way, everybody who is working hard and is skilled, must get equal opportunity for growth if the company today provides Mr. Rajat with a translator this easily then how will they define his Individual competency's parameters for reviewing his performance. The skills in question here are the presentation skills of "Mr Rajat", his personality & his communication skills required to be reviewed.

Now imagine that Mr. Rajat and Mr. P work in the same organisation, what happens next?

When Mr P. came to know a little more about the importance of these skills during the meetings & casual discussions with his manager.

What Mr P. did is no shock to me! He did not make fun of Mr. Rajat like others, neither he participated in this gossip, but he was aware of the fact that this scenario can happen with any one of us, he was able to notice the fact that this **"did not happen with him" yet.**

He experienced a growing consciousness for the need to develop the required individual competencies, irrespective of any visible opportunity he may see in front of him as of now. As he is also from the technical team, he understood that only the technical skills are not enough for him to get **extraordinary growth.**

That day when he reached home, he did research about how to develop those required skills, like his presentation in front of others, the personality he carries and his communication skills.

Mr P. was very happy to join a specific short term training course for developing these skills and spent his weekend learning those.

He literally transformed his overall personality, communication, and presentation.

2 years later after doing smarter hard work, he was sent abroad as he was the one best fit for the new project that company started, and the client really loved his working style & his AB quotient.

Further, this section needs no more details, if you understood the above scenarios and its result clearly then you understood the real meaning of the title **"Always be aware of what's NOT HAPPENING rather notice what has happened already."**

Instead of looking down on others or feeling jealous about what happened with others, have a deep understanding & awareness of what did not happen with you.

Success Principle 10

The Magical 3M Formula

Hope these scenarios & questionnaires in between the segments have kept you active and engrossed, & I hope you are able to relate yourself with each one of them. Consider it as an exercise book for your brain that will open gates for a new successful life that lies there in front of you. Just keep practising the change in approach one by one as per the given success principles, then there is nothing that you cannot achieve.

3 M's of your Life & Career

This magic of 3M's here can be applied in your career as well as in your personal life and these are the quickest way to take a leap forward in your career growth map.

Mental Satisfaction | Meaning in the work we do | Motivation

Mental Satisfaction

We learned how to find the "happy work" for ourselves in Chapter 2 under Success Principle 1 of this book.

The first M, i.e. **the mental satisfaction** is a little more than the work that just makes you happy. It is **now the manifestation stage where your work becomes your passion, and your passion becomes your life goal.**

Let us introspect again and find value in what we do!

A "value" to you should be something for which you may not receive any salary or materials in return, but you would still base your life on these beliefs and principles that directly or indirectly will be affecting someone else's life!

A person with moral values is self-motivated & whatever this person does based on these moral values gives him satisfaction.

- Shivali Tandon

This is not a medicine for the fever that you eat today & your fever is gone, to live up to these Moral Values you have to practice them each day, i.e. in every single moment, no matter if someone is looking at you or not!

Whatever we do in life, for example giving respect to others, showing empathy towards someone, or touching the feet of our parents to get their blessings, all reflect these values you have in your life.

Out of many, a few Moral values are highlighted below, and you can add more Moral Values to this list-

- Practising what we preach
- Respecting others
- Be empathetic
- Adaptability & acceptance
- Helping others
- Honesty

- Having self-discipline
- Loyalty
- Forgiveness
- Love for humanity etc. and the list goes on…

The better you can live up to your moral values while working at any organisation or in your personal life, the better is the level of your mental satisfaction.

When you start feeling satisfied mentally through your work & actions, from that day, you become a "Bigger version" of yourself. Like Tony Robbins says in his seminars that find the "giant within you", this big version of you is none other than a person who appreciates moral values and the one who believes in himself/herself.

Just for an example if your moral values are based on empathy & compassion towards others, then no matter how hard it is, you will never let injustice happen with anyone around you. You will never be at peace mentally on seeing yourself and others facing injustice or something that can hurt your nobility or dignity.

I have seen people who, without even following a single principle like the ones mentioned in this book, get a huge amount of salary, a profile, and a designation which they have not earned based on their moral values and talent but earned by adulating and buttering up to their seniors. Or by taking advantage of others at each step in their career, by using manipulative techniques, or by using their authority & power to bully someone for their own benefits.

Yes, they do have a designation and are highly paid, but during their career path, they may have lost their dignity, the respect and trust of each one they bullied or took advantage of.

Does not matter how happy they are but as they neglected the basic moral values, only their heart knows the truth that **they can never be mentally satisfied.**

Even when they are not bothered about the "mental satisfaction", they have already lost the trust of so many people they left behind to get to this point of success! But do we really appreciate such a self-seeker? Do you really call them the future leaders? Do you want to make them your mentor for life? Can they inspire you at all? I am sure and very sure that the answer is "NO".

So ultimately, all their immoral actions are zero and nobody would like to follow in the footsteps of such people even when they are the highest-paid employee in the organisation.

Always choose the right path and give it a thought whether the seed that you sow today would give you mental satisfaction tomorrow or not, your heart will never lie and will tell you the truth.

A farmer who sows the seed in the field is always mentally satisfied after successfully harvesting the crops. Do you know why? Because he is the one who performs all the right actions, starting from seed sowing, irrigation, then monitoring the crop growth, saving the crop from any damage, fertilising it and then finally he harvests the crops which give him a real sense of satisfaction.

An employee's life cycle and growth journey are nearly the same as a farmer. You must take your own responsibility to get to the last step, i.e. harvesting or as I call it the manifestation.

"Meaning" in the work we do

After getting mental satisfaction from the work that you do, it is now the time to find meaning in the work you do. Finding meaning in work is nothing but taking extra miles to make a difference for others while honouring all your moral values.

I am sure you are aware of the following media platforms: Amazon prime videos, Netflix, Hotstar etc. These platforms, other than movies & talk shows, have some amazing stuff related to science, technology, and some very amazing documentaries that will surprise you. So, a few days ago while I was watching this documentary "How to be a billionaire" on Amazon prime videos, directed by Adam Kaleta, I suddenly got attracted by one of the statements I heard in that documentary.

This is a "good to watch" documentary as it has covered the 3 richest and powerful people who would like to change the world with their vision.

I somehow was unable to understand the reason for keeping this title "How to be a billionaire," which in my view does not justify what they have shown in the documentary, but I surely loved the documentary. It showcases how someone with unique vision who is already a billionaire is working really hard to create a distinct future.

Naveen Jain is one of the 3 billionaires from the documentary. He is a business executive, entrepreneur, and the founder and former CEO of InfoSpace. InfoSpace briefly became one of the largest internet companies in the American Northwest, before the crash of the dot-com bubble and a series of lawsuits involving Jain. As per Wikipedia, he is also the Co-founder and Executive Chairman of Moon Express, and CEO of Viome.

During his interview in this documentary, a sentence he said acquired all my attention and I literally forgot about the documentary and got lost in that sentence. As I love to grasp & learn from wherever I can, this one line that I heard from Naveen Jain, I found it worth applying in my own life.

Now you see, this is how I take guidance from "INDIRECT MENTORS" as I had just mentioned above in the previous section. This statement from Naveen Jain has the same elucidation that I have for "finding meaning in the work we do".

Naveen, the father of 3 children, owns four companies and runs his own space program. He shared an incident when his elder son said to him *"you know dad, I am gonna make more money than you ever did."*

Now the reply Naveen gave to his son, is actually a very beautiful message that explains how we can find the "MEANING" in the work we do:

So, I am writing the exact words said by Naveen; he said to his son, *"You know, it is surprising! You think of success in that way. Success is not about how much money you're gonna have.* ***Success is about how many lives you'll be able to improve, and if you really want to be more successful than I am, go out and improve more people's lives than I am able to do in my lifetime, and that's what's gonna make me proud of you."***

Finding 'meaning in the work we do' has the same interpretation as mentioned by Naveen Jain. The time you will be able to make a difference in someone else's life with your work, it does not matter how big or small, you will find meaning in your work.

When you deal with people in your surroundings based upon moral values, then you already are making a difference & improving not only your life but the life of the other person in front of you. These are the basics of success.

Just to conclude here by putting all the points together about the work we do, I'll say:

We now found our "happy work" (Success Principle 1), and whatever work we do at our workplace or in our personal life, we base it upon certain moral values that give us peace & mental satisfaction. And further to find meaning to our work, we must make a difference not only in our lives but in the life of others.

If you do great work based upon above-mentioned elements, then you are helping people and then they would love to follow you & make you their mentor (direct or indirect). If you work just for yourself or for money, then people might still notice you but will never follow you as your success did not favour moral values and mental satisfaction, also it does not make any difference for others.

Motivation (The trigger)

Last but not least, the most powerful 3rd "M" is the **Motivational** factor. This motivation we need at every step of our life, as we need to relate our efforts with some motivation to never give up on ourselves.

Does the wood catch fire on its own? There needs to be a source of fire for this! This fire is called the **"trigger"**.

I know you must be pensive now thinking about taking all these actions starting today or tomorrow. Based on these principles, you are all set to make a difference in your life as well as in the life of others. But what will happen the third day or after a week, or a year when you may get stuck somewhere with a challenge in front of you. What if you will feel tired and all this hard work now appears to be tough or impossible for you to do after a few days or months or years.

Just like the gun is of no use without a "Trigger" attached to it, and so we are talking about the "trigger" of success in life, this trigger will always put your gun into the action mode. Understand it like this, that the **gun** becomes your mode of actions & efforts for success and the **trigger** becomes the motivation that will keep you going.

Proactive Approach: 10A

No matter how big the problems are, this motivation trigger will always tell you to never stop for some reasons.

Now to make it easier for you to understand, this trigger always arises from the struggle of the past or from any present condition, or anything that has hurt you the most in your life and because of it you just want to transform your life 360 degrees now!

If you want to deeply understand what trigger point is there in your life, let me share mine with you so that you can find your own trigger point (s) by relating with my situations:

1. The most important trigger point is the fact that life is too harsh, every person should put extraordinary efforts in their life to be successful, to earn money and to keep surviving in

the tough times. This trigger came from nowhere, but from my past when my mother lost her life partner, she single-handedly raised me & my sister, and trust me she did that so perfectly that I will always be having immense gratitude for the struggle she faced for both her daughters.

Had it not been her job, we could have never made it till here! That fear and that face-off with **the reality of Death** that *the one who is born will have to die, and we do not know when, where & how?* So, build this thought that every single person in our family should be capable enough to face any challenge if the family loses support from its main pillar. This was one of the reasons that I emphasise a lot on investing in education & knowledge; it gives you the best return on investment.

Till today my mother guides me to keep studying further & enhance my knowledge as vast as I can as there is no end for learning. Whichever course, training or certification I wanted to do, her answer was all the same "yes go ahead". She has always motivated me with her own struggles & experiences.

This is one of the major trigger points that pushes me each day to work hard and to find the highest potential in me. I will always miss my father, but my mother never did let me realise this as she perfectly fulfilled the role of both a father and a mother. I will be deeply indebted to her forever.

2. My second trigger point is my lovable husband, who is also my best friend. We have known each other for a decade now and recently got married in 2019. As I mentioned earlier, I was bedridden for years and had to leave my academics 2-3 times due to critical health conditions. My husband became

the trigger for me to work hard as he always wanted to see me at the top of the world, I still remember those days when he used to take me to the doctors, from one doctor to another just to see me get healthy. He never ever for a single second doubted or thought that I am incapable of anything because of my critical illness. He always comes up to me with new learning ideas as he believes in my potential that 'I can do it', and this motivates me a lot. **This trust & confidence of him is the trigger that always forces me to work hard & to prove him right.** He is supporting me in all the best ways so that I can complete my first book. Blessed to have him in my life.

3. The third & final trigger point can be a general trigger point for most of us. You are blessed to have those friends who really believe in you & your capabilities, but if sometimes a good friend or family member shows their doubt in your abilities, then that can become your trigger to achieve the impossible. It would not hurt as much if a person whom you do not like tells you that you cannot do it, rather than a close friend or family member saying this to you?? So, what did you do when they doubted your abilities, you cried the whole night and that is it? Oh no!!! That surely is not the right way. Sometimes those who care for us become the best critics and act as a catalyst to help us transform our lives. These friends and family members have pure intentions to see us grow in life.

   If you really want to be successful in life then feel that pain and let it hurt you, the more pain you feel, the more powerful your efforts will be. Now get up and make this happen!

   All those people who doubted your abilities, now your success

& unmatchable growth will be the answer to their doubts.

On a lighter note, I have seen this in a movie about a boy from a middle-class family who loved a girl so much, but she denied his proposal just because he was not successful, financially unstable and had no clear goal in his life. This **pain of rejection from her side became the trigger point in this boy's life** and instead of crying, he put his soul & heart to transform his life to become successful.

He worked so hard that towards the end of this story, we see him as a successful entrepreneur who has a spectacular personality.

Almost the same kind of situation of a daughter in another fictional story, whose father always had his doubts about her. The father loved his son so much that he did not really want her daughter to study further. But we have the power within us to change everything by changing our approach towards life. With the support, she got from her mother, this daughter in her 30's became an IPS officer with her hard work and dedication. She not only made her parents proud but is also currently supporting her family financially and helping her brother to set up his own career**. The pain she received from her father became her trigger & motivation for life!**

Isn't it so amazing! I get positive vibes after hearing such amazing transformational stories of the people around me.

So, what are you waiting for, find your trigger point, i.e. your **motivation for life?** I am confident that by having even a single trigger in your life, you can transform your life 360 degrees by following these principles or many more. This trigger will never allow you to forget even for a second that you need to change for the better.

Always remember that extreme happiness, extreme pain, or any worst failure will provide the best Triggers!

Success Principle 11

The Truth about "I" & "WE"

What do you call it & how do you really feel it?

Whenever I think of this "I" & "we" existence in one's life, it does remind me of this very popular short fable that I think my grandmother shared with me once in my childhood. It's about five brothers and their old father. I may only remember the major chunks of it, so please forgive it if it is a little different from the story you have heard. The purpose is to see which one is better "I" or "we" and most of us already know the answer, but by the end of this section we will understand how we really feel about it.

"Lesson taught by Father to his Five sons"

By doing hard work all his life, the father provided all the facilities to his five sons. As all his sons were provided with everything without even asking or without making much of an effort, they never really got to know the importance of hard work.

The father is getting old and wants to hand over the family business to his sons. He wants them to be partners with each other to continue growing his forefather's family business by taking equal actions, and **by working together as a team and** not as individual partners.

He now distributed the responsibility of the family business among his five sons based upon their knowledge, skills & age. Due to old age now, his health is deteriorating day by day and he found his five sons somehow unhappy, competing and doubting each other's potential and having a sense of ego within them.

Father was worried to see his sons becoming self-centred. They were working for a single goal, but each one of them performed their tasks with the mentality of "I". Each one of them took ownership of their respective process, but none of them was ready to accept or provide feedback to each other. They would not even share their business progress with each other.

The business was about to fall because of an increasing clash between the brothers when on a fine day the father called all his five sons and gave them a task to bring with them 2 wooden sticks each.

They all did as the father said, in no particular order, he challenged each of his sons to break a single stick with whatever strength they have in them. The sons so proudly one by one broke their respective sticks and showed their father that it was so easy for them.

Now the father collected the rest of the five sticks from them tied it in a strong knot making an unbreakable faggot and asked them to break this faggot now.

What happened next taught an important lesson to the brothers, as none of them was able to break that bunch of sticks tied together. So long story short is **that when "we" work together**, then we are more powerful, instead of standing as an individual just like the "I" which stands alone. This is what is required at the work front! TEAMWORK starts with **WE.**

The Switch from "I" to "WE"

"What we say" matters but our intent while saying something matters even more. Did you ever notice the way you write daily e-mails and messages at your workplace?

If you never thought of it earlier then next time whenever you type a message, or an e-mail then focus on the way you give out instructions in the e-mails. We will try to switch from "I" to "we" to strengthen our teamwork abilities at the workplace.

This small switch can bring about a huge impact on our working style and strengthen the bond within the team. If you think that **you can win while running alone in a relay race**, then it will be an incorrect notion, as all other hundreds and thousands of employees in the company are working for the same common goal that has been envisioned by the employer.

Imagine, I came to your company to take a short survey and personally ask questions from let us say 100 employees. I asked you this question from my list, how would you answer it? Just think about it in your mind.

My question is: What do you think the goal of your company is?

Answers will start with the statement "**Our** Goal is........."

Or

We aspire to achieve....................."

At any organisation or in your family, nothing that you do is just for yourself or to just satisfy this "I" that lies within us. You do it for a combined vision or target, be it family business or the goal of your organisation.

One cannot become an **efficient team player** by just reading about it in theory or by just preaching it with your words. Actions speak louder than words and so we need to apply the things we read and learn in real-life scenarios too.

Start developing the feeling of "WE" and it will get easier for you to inculcate the qualities of a team player, and you would be able to reflect those in your actions too. You don't have to pretend but need to develop this feeling from within that "we are a team", "we" are one and are working hard together to accomplish a common larger goal. Try this and the "I" in you will reap the benefit of it too.

Proactive Approach: 11A

A couple of qualities that will make you a great team player:

- An effective team player is committed to the success of its team and is ready to contribute as much as possible.
- Effective team player is most reliable and takes responsibility for the collaborative work assigned as a team.
- Very adaptive and flexible in accepting the change that can result in success.
- Always protect themselves & the team from politics.
- They spread the magic of "appreciation" within the team by always appreciating the co-workers for their working style.
- Always keeps the information as transparent & clear as possible amongst the co-workers so that every individual within the team is on the same page.

- Team player never is worried to take extra efforts to help someone within the team as he looks at the work as a collaborative project that results in success.
- He is a problem solver who never sits quietly if the team is taking a wrong path, team players always come with a plan that is acceptable to all and can bring about the desired result.

The five brothers who thought they were just "I" now aligned themselves towards the common goal & came together under the shelter of "WE". Same is the situation at our workplace, the "I" that lies within us aligns itself with a bigger goal of the company & we naturally become housed under the common roof of "WE".

So ultimately, we work as an individual but represent ourselves as "WE" by polishing the hidden "I" that lies within, i.e. while performing as a team for a common goal, whatever rewards & recognition we receive in return provides benefit to this "I" individual that lies within us.

The impact on "Success" as a Team player vs Individual contributor

Model: 11B

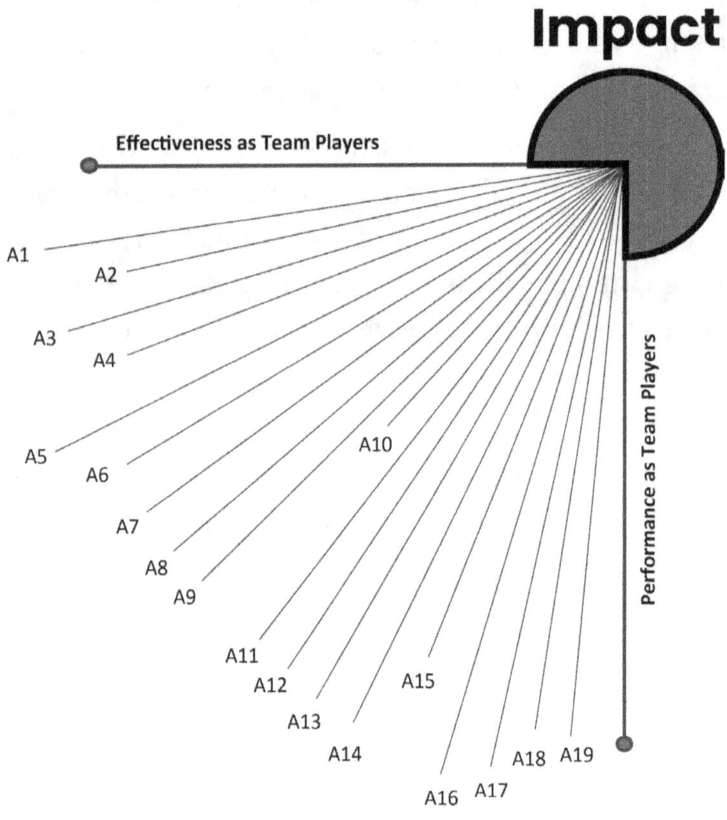

Team A includes 19 members of effective TEAM PLAYERS, all with various skills, performance, and grades. It really does not matter if team member "A10" joined this project late or has fewer skills as compared to others, rest 18 members will ensure he reaches to the final goal with them sharing the same impact. The impact can be seen at the point where variant skills and ideas collaborate while focussing at one goal. Team members "A5", or "A16" or "A17" with highest skills & experience will surely put extra efforts to make sure everybody gets to the success point with the same impact as a TEAM.

Polishing the "I" - Individual contributor within us

Time for a quick exercise and you will surely pick the correct option if you really understood the concept of switching from "I" to "We". I will give you a scenario and 2 options for expressing your thoughts. Choose any 1 option out of the 2 in each scenario or simply notice the difference between both the opinions.

1st scenario:

You were asked to complete one report for which you need to collect details from your subordinate, this report further needs to be sent to your manager within 1 hour and further he needs to send it to the Sr. management for some critical work that needs to be closed.

Which e-mail expresses the "WE" element and how will the sender display this in the e-mail to his subordinate, so that he (the sender) gets all the required data that must be compiled for the final draft.

Option A:

Hi (Recipient's name),

Please note that I need to send the PQR report to Josef (the manager) by 4 PM today.

I need the specifics on this from you for final compilations of the data as this needs to be sent further to Sr management.

Please complete this before 3:30 PM.

Thanks & Regards

Sender's name

Option B:

Hi (Recipient's name),

This is regarding the PQR report that is required by Josef (the manager) today and **we are targeting** to further send this report **to our** Sr management.

Josef has requested to fill in the details that **are available with us.** Kindly share the details that are available with you so that a consolidated report can be prepared & sent to Josef.

Let us try to complete this before 3:30 PM.

Thanks & Regards

Sender's name

In option B the sender is surely emphasising on the importance of the report but at the same time informing the recipient (his subordinate) that **we need to complete it together.** Although the sender will have to work alone for the final draft, towards the end of the e-mail he makes sure not to command his subordinate in authority rather he showed his subordinate the shared aim of completing this task by writing "**LET US** try to complete this before 3:30 PM" instead of giving a command as per Option A -

"Please complete this by 3:30 PM".

2nd scenario:

The Sr. management of the organisation is working on some strategic analysis and have requested each Team leader to share the SWOT analysis of their department. The SWOT analysis is a way to analyse the Strengths, Weaknesses, Opportunities, and Threats of a person or the whole team. The management has requested the team leads to take suggestions from everyone before sending this final draft to them.

One of the team members is on a short leave during the first half of the day and the manager has asked another team member to coordinate with her about the SWOT analysis requirement regarding their department and share her points as soon as she joins back after her half-day leave...

Also, the same team member has got this responsibility to collect SWOT analysis data from each team member to send a consolidated report to the team leader.

Text message:

Option A

Hey, "Name"!

Hope you are fine.

I have received a request from the team lead to consolidate the SWOT analysis for our department.

Every team member, including you, will have to share their

suggestions to get to the final analysis.

Please make sure to share your suggestions & analysis points with me as soon as you join in today after your short leave is over.

Thank you! Bye.

Option B:

Hey, "Name"!

Hope you are fine. Sorry to bother you during your short leave, please consider this just an information message as we all need to send our SWOT analysis representing our department.

Our team leader has given me the responsibility to collect individual's data within the team so that a consolidated SWOT analysis report can be sent to the management for our department.

It would be great if you can send your suggestions to me once you join in for the day.

Thanks, Take care!

Bye :)

When you use "I" and "you" while giving orders, it shows your authoritative attitude as the manager chose you from your team to prepare a consolidated report. You cannot be showing this authoritative behaviour to others.

If any task is given specifically to you, irrespective of what designation or grade you have, you should consider it as a "Responsibility". Please note that we are not talking about the KRA's assigned to any individual, rather we are talking about the responsibility given to you on behalf of the whole team. The way you request the information from the colleagues and subordinates impacts your teamwork element here.

Everybody is clearly aware of the work assigned to everyone within the team, if you are approaching someone for a piece of information and explaining it clearly that **"WE" need to complete this for the team and as a team, then your colleague will understand it anyhow.**

Prefer to use **"Let us try** to complete this task" instead of "do this work by 5 PM" or "you have to share this with me". These are just a couple of examples on how to shift from "I" to "we" approach. Your team members will never feel offended when you use more of the terms "WE", "let us", "let us do it", "We have to do it", "We need to share this", even if only you have to complete that task alone!

Try it and in the long-term, this shift will have a magnificent effect on your career growth, and it will strengthen your bonding within the team.

Fruits & the failure

Scenario:

A manufacturing company plans to launch a new product, numerous employees with various skills are involved till the final launch of the product, starting from the concept preparation to the final manufacturing & the launch. Can a product be launched successfully only by a single individual? Of course not, it will be a shared effort by each of the involved stakeholders.

When the product is launched successfully, then appreciation is given to each one of the stakeholders. Be it the designer, or someone who did the research, someone who converted the idea into a 3D model with the help of computer-aids, to someone who did the testing of the product, someone who manufactured it or to someone one who assembled it. None of the steps can be ignored, as each step is important for the best outcome.

Fruits of success of a successful product launch are shared amongst all the associates as it is always a team effort and not just an individual effort.

But do we take responsibility as a team **when we encounter a failure?**

So, shifting from the "I" approach to the "WE" approach also includes this element where **the fruits and failures are shared equally.** Do not worry as there is no harm in doing that. Stop using these statements: I didn't do it; he did it, you did it, they did it etc.

In case of any failure during the manufacturing process, how about saying it like so,

*"Surely it was a miss from **our side** & **we agree** that there is a scope of improvement here".*

We do not have to specify the mistake or need to take any individual's name as every stakeholder will have somewhat of an idea as to wherein lies the issue. We should never embarrass the team or department or even an individual during the discussions and meetings where the failures are being discussed. What is done is done, try to focus on the next step that how the modification or revision can be done.

At the time of performance review, let the manager decide how much score he needs to reduce against the failures one has encountered. To save the team member from any embarrassment, such issues are addressed during one-on-one performance meetings or during a normal face to face meeting with this individual who is responsible for the failure.

• Dispersal of Rewards being "I"

Imagine that your performance during a team project was so great that you were rewarded as the "employee of the month". Now think about those who were associated with you during the work, the victory is surely yours and so is the award, but it would not cost you a single penny to show your gratitude to the rest of the team who really worked hard with you on this project. Not all can get "Employee of the month" award, but a sense of gratitude and acknowledgement will surely boost the team's energy. Share your reward with all your team members just like a team player who moves up on the ladder by holding other's hands.

This is the way of distributing the rewards being "I" that lies within us all this time.

• Dispersal of Pressure being "We"

When rewards can be shared, then why not the work pressure?

When you have completed the task assigned to you, then help the other person who is stuck or is behind schedule in completing his task. Ultimately the goal is to provide the best service to the client or an end-user as a team so that we can add value to the larger goal that the company has envisioned.

If it is possible and is in your capacity, then always be ready to share the work pressure within your team.

If any team member needs help to complete his or her own task for timely work delivery, then never hesitate in providing the necessary assistance.

Wisdom is something that plays a lot of roles here, as you cannot allow a clever or lazy co-worker to take advantage of you being supportive and helping all the time. So, it will be your wisdom and heart that will help you in determining this and about how much support you need to provide to this person.

Success Principle 12
Information sharing

Not to be thought of as a principle, it is basically a technique about information sharing and how information is the most powerful tool that we have with us, but only when we use it correctly. It can become a curse if shared with the wrong person and at any incorrect time.

Written information Vs Verbal information

Whenever a decision is made, or any issue is resolved, it should all be present in writing with you, preferably in e-mails as you never know when this written information will be of use in future.

For any internal or external communication to be done, it is always better to maintain records via e-mails on the information you collect or share verbally on a day-to-day basis.

We all know the benefits of e-mail communication and how it saves time, fast and easy to communicate, but apart from that, e-mails are the reliable form of communication between the parties.

Verbal information can be omitted easily, but written information once recorded can never be lost.

Always write in an e-mail whatever has been decided during

the meetings, as we sometimes prefer to hold on to this verbal information without ever penning it down due to a lot of work & busy schedules. This verbal information could be an important decision, your next target for the project, any agreement or disagreement, any acknowledgement, or any client requirement etc.

If anybody leaves the organisation, no one calls the ex-employee after a year to confirm what was decided during the meeting?

In some cases, the culprit is our memory, as everybody tries to best memorise what had been discussed and what were the agreeable points, but none of us recorded those points in an e-mail and then suddenly after 6 months when the management asked for the status or last decision made upon any work/ assignment, we have lost that very important information as none of us now remember that. It would have been a different scenario if someone within the team had recorded even the smallest information in an e-mail.

Fake information

This is the worst form of the information and what is said by someone randomly cannot always be true. You listen to something and are shocked or surprised, and you just go running to that someone who might find this piece of information very relevant and you share it with him. What if the information comes out to be fake? Someone just misled you with the information. Be a good listener, stay alert and let your mind absorb everything that is being said and done but does not spread out everything you hear as you are not sure of its impact and authenticity.

Your wisdom plays an important role in collecting & sharing any information, be wise and save yourself from any fake information misleading.

Confidential information

Confidential information is the best tool to determine the trust factor of someone. People sometimes fail to secure confidential information shared with them within the organisation or outside the organisation. Give respect to the trust that someone has shown on you when sharing something confidential with you that might impact a large group of people.

As you go higher in the organisational hierarchy, then almost every single bit of information that you know becomes highly confidential. You need to be very sure about what impact it may have on the person if he/she is exposed to something confidential that only you know.

Let the actual source share this information with a group of people. You must not violate the most important code of conduct related to the security of the information.

For example:

You heard about a process that is getting closed soon in your company and this may result in too many layoffs, this information should be shared by a concerned authority to a group of members at the right time and place.

Somehow you could not resist your shock & concern about this information, you go straight to your colleague or friend and tell him everything and request him not to tell this further to anyone. If you could not resist your concern, then how can you expect the other person to hold onto that confidential information, **the information once shared will spread and that is for sure.**

In the worst scenarios, the source of information is easily exposed. The person who has spread this important information has to face serious consequences for violating the basic code of conduct. Also, you can become the reason for extreme panicky situations amongst the team members as nobody wants to go through a layoff and this has created fear amongst the team members. This is one simple example, but there are different types of information at each level that **demands your commitment to confidentiality.**

As a top performer, you must always stay away from such complications. Confidential information is just like a powerful weapon till the time it is secure with you, let it out at the right time & only through concerned authorities. It might cause a lot of damage if the wrong kind of people gets their hands on it at the wrong time.

Success Principle 13

It is ok to make mistakes & it is best to accept the actual one!

Nobody likes to make mistakes in life! It is a very basic human tendency that not everybody likes to accept their mistakes.

Mistakes can be small or big, done individually or in a group, and ultimately it creates a lot of pressure and tension in the life of the person who did it.

Mistakes and failures are part of life and anyone who works hard can commit mistakes or may face failure. **The realisation of these mistakes makes us what we are today, i.e. a better version than yesterday** and with hope not to repeat the same mistake again we aspire to be a better version of self, for tomorrow.

Embrace the failure & let go of the pain - Activity: 13A -

Let's do a small activity that will heal any past regrets or pain that is there in your heart which reminds you of the mistakes you made or failures you have faced. Do as mentioned step by step as it will take only 2 minutes.

Close your eyes for 1minute and take 3 deep breaths while focusing your attention on the breath, feeling the breathing in, and breathing out. Do it and then open your eyes to read the next part.

Now again close your eyes and **think of the 3 best things you ever did in your life successfully.** It can be any small or big event, or a surprise was given to someone, or when you helped someone, or when you got recognition at the workplace for your extraordinary performance. Now close your eyes and think about these 3 things and come back to read the next section of this.

You must be feeling a bit happy now about your actions that you were able to bring about a difference in your life or in the life of others. Now close your eyes for one last **time to think of 3 mistakes or failures that have hurt you the most, or that mistake that has affected someone else's life and if you have any regrets for it.**

This time when you will close your eyes while imagining about 3 mistakes or failures of your life, you do not have to open your eyes immediately.

We are **freeing our soul, heart and mind from any mistake or failure that we regret.** Your soul, thoughts, and creativity are like birds that have wings, but cannot fly as the wings have been crushed under the burden of these regrets & failures.

Tell yourself in your heart:

"I learnt something from these mistakes and failures. I free myself today from all the regrets and hopelessness that had developed inside me.

I am determined not to repeat the same mistake again and I am determined to transform my failure into success again."

If you are not able to say these lines with closed eyes, that is ok, you can read these lines with open eyes, but **make sure you feel the emotion behind this exercise.**

Let's do it! With the help of this exercise, you are allowing yourself to free yourself from any pain or regret pertaining to your failures or mistakes.

Use this technique whenever you encounter any failure or make any mistake in life. Embrace them by taking them as an opportunity to improve yourself and become a better version for tomorrow.

Acceptance

The toughest element is to accept our mistakes. Usually, we immediately try to defend ourselves when we get pinpointed about our mistake by our manager or someone else. It is human tendency to present the best possible reasons because of which the mistake has occurred.

We cannot undo it by going back in the past, but we can change it now for the present & future that lies ahead of us.

You would surely be able to comprehend as to which was the mistake, that was made by you and which mistake is blame that is being put upon you. We are not talking about the intentions here; a **mistake is a mistake with or without the intentions**. A mistake is not a mistake when it is manipulatively or politically put as blame on you; in such cases, you must not accept it at all.

It is ok to make mistakes & it is best to accept the actual one! Do not lie to yourself; there is no benefit in making yourself happy for a moment by denying your actual mistake, as you will surely lose this opportunity to learn from that mistake.

"A Failure & Mistake can become a learning opportunity only when you are ready to accept it positively, and when you make sure that you do not repeat the same mistake again and again".

- Shivali Tandon

To transform our Mistakes/Failures into Learning & Opportunity Model: 13B

This is one of the best ways that I found while I was working upon how to **de re-motivate** myself after noticing my mistakes and failures. The impact of these mistakes and failures is so heavy upon us that it affects our performance for future challenges as we are left with so many doubts and confusions in our mind.

These **3 stages will save you from getting caught up by this perplexity** and surely will work without fail; the only thing required is the correct approach.

This transformation is a little different where **we do not get a choice to accept this transformation or reject it,** in reality, **this transformation accepts us or rejects** us by seeing our positive approach to getting to our long-term career goal.

Stage 1

Stage of Realisation and Introspection

The stage at which we are made aware of our mistake, through our manager, friend, or family member.

Let us think about the mistake/failure and introspect where the loophole exists. After introspection, you will immediately understand that yes, it was your mistake or the reason behind the failure of a particular task or project. You did not reach to the **"Expected envisioned goal"** & now standing at the point of **"Reality"** in this stage (as shown in the graph 13B1). This realization is important so that necessary actions can be taken to overcome the problem.

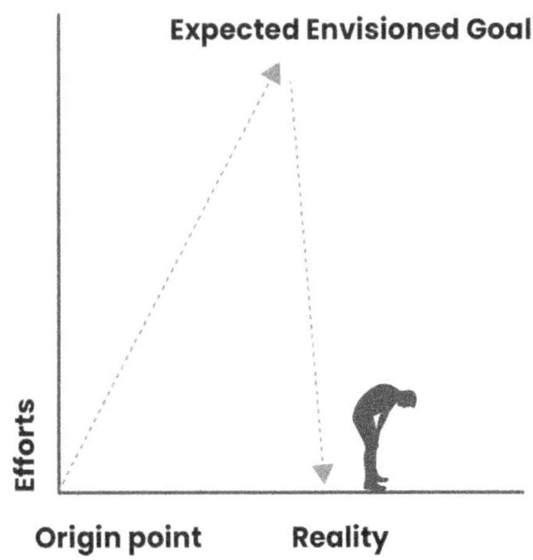

13 B1 "Stage of Realization"

For more benefits, it will be great if you become a good listener & first listen to the concerned party who is explaining your mistake or discussing your failure. Try to understand how it has affected not only your work but had its impact on the whole team.

This person will always be more experienced & senior to you in the hierarchy. Respect their thoughts and allow them to share their level of experience relevant to that mistake or failure, as there is no harm at all if we simply listen to this person. Maybe the heart does not want to agree with all the points he/she mentioned, but a calmly done discussion and introspection always give birth to a better thought and future experience.

Stage 2

Stage of Bouncing Back

Not every time we are lucky enough to have a manager, friend or person around us who calmly explains our faults and helps us understand their point of views. This person may end up shouting at you because of the mistake as he may not be having a positive AB quotient like you and is unable to balance between harshness and formal tone. In such a case, after getting an earful from this person for your mistake or failure may literally break your heart and **you might enter a dull phase.**

'Stage of Bouncing back' is to pick up only the useful points out of this discussion by maintaining a positive AB Quotient and focussing only on the L-N-E facts. This is the time to learn from these mistakes and failures.

By defending and arguing with this experienced person, just

because I do not like the way he/she has conveyed my mistake to me, will bring me nothing but only disappointment. Maybe the more you try to defend yourself, the more annoyed the other person becomes, so whatever had to happen, just happened and you will have to deal with the present & future now.

Sometimes you need to walk down the rough path in order to reach your destination, just like hiking to the top of the mountain, you might get too tired and your feet might get sore, but once you reach the top, the view from up is just exceptionally beautiful and worth it.

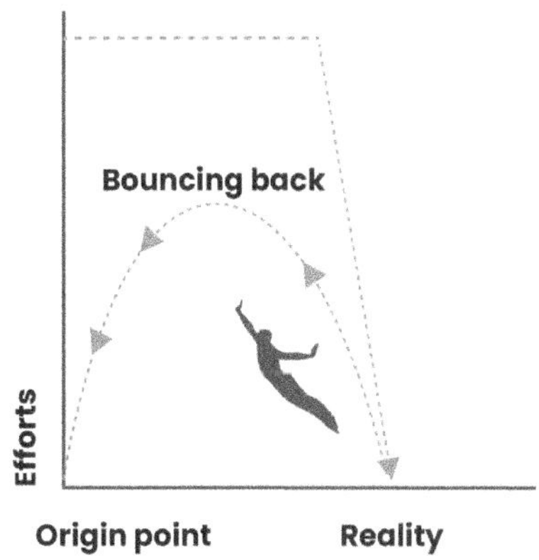

13 B2 "Stage of Bouncing Back"

As shown in the graph, we should dust off the disappointment and start our journey again with the same zeal from the **Origin point**. **Do not let yourself get stuck up in this moment of failure.**

You surely are hurt and regretting the situation in front you, but you need to **BOUNCE BACK** to keep learning from your mistakes and not to repeat the same mistake again.

We have already experienced the technique for bouncing back to normal, close your eyes and think 3 best things you ever did, now think of this particular mistake, ask yourself what you have learnt from this failure or mistake and then let go of the pain with a deep breathing exercise. In the upcoming section, Success Principle 18: "You as the Powerhouse", we will learn how to activate this "Energy" that is there within us that helps us face such small & big failures more conveniently without any pain & sorrow by **meeting our true self.**

Stage 3

The final Stage: Transformation

So, the impact on the result is much more magnificent as compared to the initial result we were expecting. When we make mistakes or fail once or twice, we become more cautious while taking further steps that can lead to success. **The bouncing back from the failures or from your mistakes will be an amazing experience** as you will become more powerful & optimistic every time you bounce back.

The 2nd stage, i.e. **the bouncing back is very important & that is the only exit gate you can use to overcome the pain & regrets you have after a failure or after seeing the effects of your own mistakes.**

<u>**This whole process and its 3 stages will keep on repeating itself until and unless you succeed and transform yourself by learning from your failures & mistakes.**</u> The same principle is applicable in your personal life. Remember these stages & whenever you regret a failure in life, just bounce back again &

again from where you started and make as many attempts as possible to get to the finest result. It is a never-ending transformation process.

Bouncing Back Transformational Model: 13B

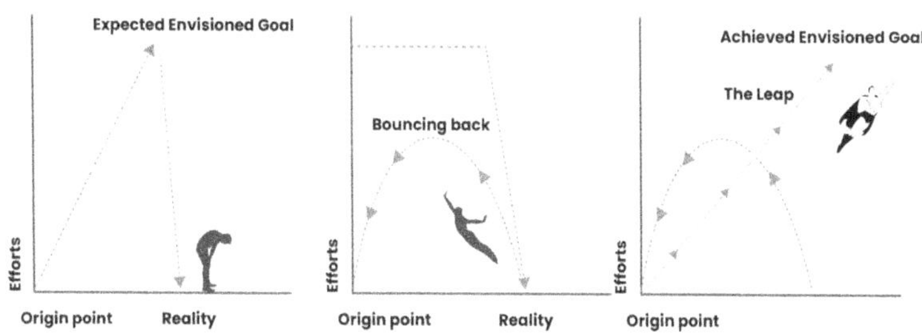

13 B1 "Stage of Realization" 13 B2 "Stage of Bouncing Back" 13 B3 "Transformation"

After repeated attempts of "Bouncing Back" at the 2nd stage (13 B2), ultimately as you can see in the **last stage (13 B3)** you finally take "The Leap" and achieve "The envisioned goal".

Success Principle 14

"The OBCD" long-term Career planner

Let's come to another scenario.

Ms. Tanya went for an interview. Towards the end of the interview, the interviewer asked her, where do you see yourself after 5 years or 10 years down the line?

She failed to answer this question satisfactorily and lost the Job. The interviewer was looking for a person who had a clear vision and knew where the candidate wants to see himself after 5 or 10 years.

Those employees who envision clearly where they will be after 5 to 10 years on their career roadmap are the employees who become the most valued associates within the company.

They clearly share their expectation by answering this question precisely and the employer is also able to merge the company's vision with that of the employee's so that maximum benefit can be obtained by both the parties.

The employer puts the rewards on the table to make this employee's vision a reality & the employee in return performs extraordinarily to help the organisation to achieve its vision. This is what I call the "**intersecting point**" where the goal of the company & the goal of the employee meet each other at a common point, creating value for each other's success.

I also once encountered a similar question during an interview and unfortunately, I did not have a clear answer for it at that point of time, but today I have the answer as I have worked upon formulating my long-term career plan and I am aware of how I need to achieve it. After finding **my "happy work" and "3 M's" of life, i.e. the purpose and meaning of the work I do, now I surely have a very clear vision**. This helps me to align my personal career growth plan with the success of the organisation through smarter hard work and self-upgradation as per latest trends.

Always remember if the organisation grows due to an employee's hard work & honesty, then the employee also grows along with it and bears fruit for his hard work in terms of good hikes and promotions.

The OBCD - long-term career planner Model: 14A

Basically, we are depicting the career journey of an employee in the below diagram. At some point of time in his career, we see him as a lead handling a team of capable resources, then after 10 years, we see him as a manager leading several projects in his organisation. He worked hard, upgraded his skills to stand out from the crowd, and kept following his dreams to get to this intersecting point.

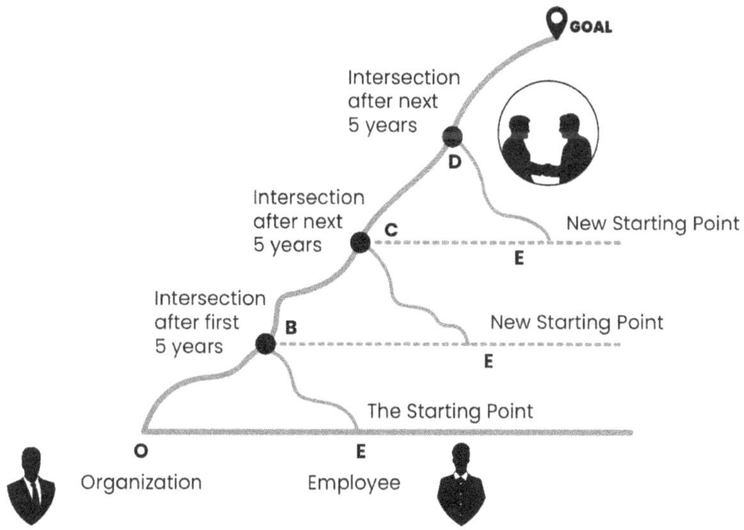

Base your CAREER PLAN on this OBCD planner as shown above

Interpretation of the diagram

- **The wavy lines** depict the ups & down one faces during the journey.
- **O** - Organisation
- **E** - Employee (you)
- **B** - Where the company's & Employee's goals meet successfully after the first five years (or less) of Employee's career.
- **C** - Where the company's & Employee's goals meet successfully after the next five years of the Employee's career with a new starting point that employee reached upon after the first five years.
- **D** - Where the company's & Employee's goals meet successfully

after the next five years of Employee's career with a new starting point that had been established after the first 10 years (or less).

- **Goal** - It is the point where both the Organization & its employees want to reach to accomplish something extraordinary.
- **Black dot** - "The intersection growth point" where the organisation & employee meet by working together towards a common goal.
- **The Starting Point** - This point after each intersection becomes a fresh start for example: New plans & next level goal setting for achieving the subsequent intersection.

If you successfully learn to work through this OBCD Career planner, then your success is guaranteed along with the success of the organisation. It really does not matter how many organisations you change during your career; these intersections are purely based upon the employee's long-term career plan he/she creates.

Your goals should be checked after every 5 years (or less) and you must make sure to work dedicatedly towards this goal that is aligned with the goal of the organisation and after every 5 years (or less) there must be an intersection point at which both you and the organisation were able to achieve their respective **"Extraordinary goal"** that had been set for those 5 years.

Every time you reach the intersection point, i.e. the "black dot" in the diagram, it becomes the new starting point from where you revisit your growth speed or any shortcomings. You then replenish your long-term plan with more defined & clear vision so that the next intersection after further 5 years down the line becomes even more significant and impactful. When I say impactful, it simply means to add greater value to your own success as well to the success & growth of the company.

How to define your long-term career plan based on the "OBCD model"?

Get clarity by sincerely exploring the things that are mentioned below. We have learnt some of these already in previous sections:

1. Know your **Happy work**
2. Make the 3M's your power to become extraordinary - **Mental Satisfaction**, Finding **Meaning** in the work you do & **Motivational Trigger**.
3. Deeply understand what **company's goal & values** are - if you are not clear about it, **do not wait**, someone authorised and senior in the system will be happy to share this with you.
4. **Find what skills you lack** for this meaningful work as per the latest market trends.
5. **Find the intersecting point**- write it down somewhere that where do you see yourself after 5 years & then after more 5 years and so on. Think about having 1 or 2 extraordinary intersections between the first 10 years of your career. This interaction can be noticed if you get a promotion, a reward, and a growth opportunity in the organisation by exhibiting the required skills & knowledge along **with smarter hard work.**
6. **Take every <u>ethical action</u> in your capacity to get to this intersection.**

7. The vision of the company, of course, is huge, massive and you must find a point where your vision intersects with that of the company's after every 5 years (or less) as per the plan you envisioned.

These Interactions are very important and can have an exemplary impact on your growth. Set designations, profile, job grade & targets for yourself as per OBCD model, as this plan will be the answer to the question that the interviewer asked Ms. Tanya "where do you see yourself after 5 or 8 or 10 years down the line".

So where do you see yourself after 5 or 10 years and what all you need to do to reach that level, is a question that everybody should ask themselves? **The answer to this question will allow your personal growth goals to intersect smoothly with the Goals of the company.**

Success Principle 15

That last breath...

I am confident and I do believe in you that you will be able to implement each of the elements in your daily life to open-up gates for limitless opportunities and growth in your career as well life.

So, we know by now that the responsibility is ours and only ours to see this change and to implement the change correctly.

But there are a few things that cannot be changed only from one side, for it to be changed; the implementation is required from both sides. If the disagreement is shown from any one side to accept this change, then things would never be cordial between these two parties. Except for this one change that can never be accomplished without 2nd person's agreement or efforts, rest all the changes can be done & you can witness the positive impact in your surroundings as well.

I am referring here to a "person-specific change", this person is not only different but also very tough to deal with.

The title of this section is "The last breath", not relating to death, but it is the last breath of sigh, languish or hopelessness.

We try hard to make any relationship healthy & smooth by encouraging each other and out of these 100 people whom you encourage each day, **there can be one person who is extremely tough to handle & deal with.**

I personally believe in never giving up on any person easily until I met this one specific person, i.e. my colleague who was so different and unexpected.

Even after so many efforts to make things better between us as formal co-workers, I failed to see the slightest change or agreement from his side on my efforts.

If this 1 person does not exist in your surroundings, then you are really very lucky, do keep encouraging people and lead by example. If you have found this person and have no option but to work closely with him/her at the office or in personal life, then try to stay calm as deep down in your heart you do know your efforts can go in vain as this person doesn't want to change at all.

Let me share one small fictional story here with imaginary characters:

There are 2 boys "Sam" & "Jackson" they both work under one team. At the same job levels, but different age, having the same goals but different work APPROACH.

Both have targets to achieve 5 new sales every month, or if you are in any other industry, you can imagine any 5 targets you & your team members have to fulfil every month.

Sam is already practising these success principles daily and is amongst the top performers in the team; his focus is very clear; he respects others and expects the same respect in return from others. He is ready to help and share whatever knowledge he has; he is flexible and adaptable. With a remarkable **AB quotient and L-N-E attentiveness,** he is already ways ahead of the rest of the team members irrespective of his age & years of experience, as he is a very **quick learner**, always ready to **accept his actual mistake**

& bounce back immediately after encountering a failure in life. This is what we have learnt so far and this is what makes us an extraordinary performer.

Jackson, on the other side, is the opposite of Sam, Jackson is older than Sam, but in the organisational hierarchy, he is 1 grade below Sam. Jackson has faced some critical failures in life, some major losses in his life and **he missed to bounce back on time which has caused him to be a terrible performer at the office and in his personal life.** He can love you for a second and can make you his enemy too in the very next second after that. He can be the worst manipulative person you could have ever met.

Sam & Jackson will have to work under the same team. By giving the benefit of the doubt for Jackson's age and his struggles, Sam always forgives him for his unethical behaviour within the team.

Sam knew that Jackson lies to him, that Jackson easily gets jealous with him as he is amongst the top performers. Jackson, instead of focusing on his own life Goals, always focusses when & how Sam is being recognised. For example, if Sam & Jackson work on a report, then Jackson wants to take all its credit in Sam's absence. Jackson argues with Sam and during conflict management, by literally telling lies uses manipulative statements.

Whatever Sam receives in reward of good work, Jackson competes for it. Sam many times sat down with Jackson and encouraged him to find this positive power that we all have inside of us that helps us to get rid of negative thoughts, ugly competition and hopelessness, but somehow all his efforts were in vain.

Sometimes Jackson smiles & shows a lot of care & love for

Sam, but later or sooner, Sam always came to know that it was all fake. Jackson congratulates Sam for his promotion but in a very sarcastic tone. Sam, being so connected with universal powers, is always able to sense the truth about Jackson's actions. It surely hurts when we try our level best, to help someone to get better, to share with them our own secrets of success, but in return instead of showing gratitude, they bully you.

Do you have a "Jackson" in your team or in personal life? If yes. Then you need to take him very seriously as he can become the biggest distraction and hindrance in your life.

The lies of Jackson became torture for Sam; sometimes, Sam felt so suffocated that he was not able to perform well at work. Sam's hope for seeing Jackson as a good friend and as a better colleague was getting dull day after day.

Jackson started doing small talks about Sam and it was tough for Sam to hold on to his anger anymore. Sam became negative and hopeless. If someone focuses on small talks about others, then they get too distracted to succeed in their own life and Jackson was one such person.

Can you see the impact, this one person shook Sam's peace of mind & his strength with repeated bullying? That was the day Sam took his last breath of hopelessness. This hopelessness was not for himself, but for Jackson. Sam literally felt pity for Jackson for not being able to focus on his own life & career, for his manipulative techniques to keep pulling down other's legs in the race of career growth.

Competition is good when it is healthy and is fair for both the parties; it should not hurt any of the parties. We should always hold on to the mentality of 'may the best man win'.

That day Sam decided to draw an unerasable line between him & Jackson. He stopped talking to him and did not respond to his lies or manipulative talks as Jackson knew this was the only way he could provoke Sam and distract him from performing well.

Sam used his "SILENCE" as a weapon against Jackson; this silence can indirectly threaten people like Jackson not to cross their limits.

People like Jackson are not worth fighting with words and there is no point of proving them wrong for their worst actions. *When you become silent you just throw the ball in the other person's court and turn around showing your disinterest to play anymore; also you give no reason as to why you took this exit, this surprises the other person, and he loses the battle anyhow.*

A situation like that of Sam is very rare & there is one in a thousand chance that we get to meet such an impossible personality. **Use this weapon only when it's the dead end and there is no hope of improvement from the other side**. Save your energy for your success and start following your routine of working hard smartly by ignoring people like Jackson.

Answer them with no words to stop them from creating an issue out of anything you say. Maintain distance from such negative, manipulative people. Do whatever is best as part of the code of conduct to complete collaborative tasks with this person. Make sure you do it all in writing with valid proof of work, by doing so, you save yourself from getting into an unnecessary or provoking argument.

Sam knew that no more discussions could help to make this relationship better. So, he stopped seeing him. If they had a task to perform together, he changed his way of working, and kept every interaction short, to the point and on e-mails for his own records, so that at a later stage Jackson is no longer able to tell lies about the work done.

There will be moments when you will give up on some people and will take this last breath of languish & hopelessness. It is ok to sometimes save your energy and to not to try to make a lot of extra effort for this person.

This should not mean that you start considering everyone around you as Jackson as people like Jackson are rare, very rare. Use your wisdom and do not do injustice with a genuine person by giving up on him. Even Jackson had some bad experiences in his life that made him this harsh & deceitful. Someday, Jackson, would himself be able to figure out the do's & don'ts. Sam can inspire someone with his own success, but he cannot really become Jackson's Guru or mentor here as the "ACCEPTANCE" element is missing from Jackon's side.

Actually, people like Jackson are the one who helps you learn a lot, had it not been these challenges and hurdles they created for you, you would never have had the chance to bounce back & develop yourself.

By doing this, Sam found a tougher & a better version of himself. He did not allow any small talk or manipulations to affect his performance. Sam knew how to remove this distraction and save himself from getting deviated from his "long-term career goal".

Success Principle 16

The L-O-C, where is our Line of Control?

Have you ever tried to calm down two parties while they were fighting, just like a referee does in a boxing match?

It's an awesome feeling when two members who are fighting or arguing, suddenly give up the fight by agreeing to your suggestion and you were able to facilitate this patch up between these two members.

Have you ever noticed, if during a boxing match the fighters lose their composure and stop following the rules, then the referee needs to step-in to resolve this conflict, and he might easily get hurt while trying to do so? He still can manage it, as it is part of his job, but our job in real life is not to be guiding over fights & patch-ups at the workplace.

Imagine that any one of your teammates asked you to pick a side while you were trying to sort out their argument or fight by being a mediator. You will end up losing all your energy in getting out of this dilemma and might even hurt your relationship with one or both of your teammates.

You are not a referee for patch-ups!

Suggestions should be given when the point of view matches. For 2 different people who obviously fight with each other because of a different point of views, it is simple that there is no middle path for it.

One person will have to win, and the other person will have to lose the battle. At the end of it, you may lose a friend, colleague, and a team member if you pick a side.

Fight for something that is really worth it, do not become a referee, take your stand for either side or for none, i.e. stand against injustice if it is happening, rather than trying to help people to reconcile after a worthless argument.

This is another important element that helps you maintain a good relationship with those around you. If your AB quotient is good, and you have worked upon your personality development and have decided your long-term goal as per "OBCD planner" then you are soon about to become a better version of yourself. So, it is better not to get involved in these arguments, discussions and fights that are not at all related to you.

Your suggestions & time have some value, give it to those who really can bring about some change in their life. Maybe one of the 2 parties has a valid point, and you want to support the first member but why to lose the trust of another member. A smart person always knows how to remain neutral all the time.

Stay away from such arguments that can involve you as a third person without any reason. **You may weaken your potential and focus by getting involved in these issues.** Also, you may worsen the situation just in case any 1 of the colleague/friend has strong bonding with you & you will be in a dilemma to choose one of the sides and surely it would be very wrong to act partially!

Let us understand this with a Scenario:

Let's say Mr. Smith tries to sort the issue between Nitesh and Akshay, at the coffee table during an evening work break - **Akshay is a very good friend of Mr. Smith, but** Mr. Smith has a good rapport with both the colleagues. Now **Nitesh has concerns with Akshay** regarding him not sharing proper data & hiding important information from Nitesh because of competition or what not!

While Akshay & Nitesh are arguing on this issue, Mr. Smith is trying to understand the issue & thinking ways to sort it out, suddenly Akshay who is a good friend of Mr. Smith asks him.

"Smith please tell all of us that this is a very wrong blame Nitesh is putting on me... Do you really think that I can hide any important information or data from anyone? I always send you and everybody the best possible details I have."

Now try to understand the perspective of Akshay here that he is actually sharing all the required details with Mr. Smith, in fact, he is even sharing all those details as well that are not part of Mr. smith's work as he considers him to be a very good friend of his. But maybe his terms are not that good with Nitesh, and what if Akshay explicitly is not sharing the data with Nitesh?

If Mr. Smith now agrees with Akshay, which in actual will be an honest answer, and as being his good friend, it is true that Akshay never hides anything from Mr. smith.

On the other side, Nitesh may be surprised as Mr. Smith is supporting Akshay. **Nitesh may also be right** for sharing his concern as due to Akshay's poor terms with him, Akshay may not be sharing all the required information with him as a team member.

You really do not know the truth here, as you have a good relationship with both the parties. If Mr. Smith does not say anything then obviously Akshay, who is a very good friend with Mr. Smith may begin to doubt their relationship and friendship.

In both cases, Mr. Smith would get stuck between this argument from nowhere. **The focus from the actual argument has now been shifted on to Mr. Smith and his answer.** This argument may never end, but Mr. Smith surely is losing either a friend or a colleague today!

I hope you got my point; your approach should be clear while getting involved in unnecessary arguments and discussions.

Provide space to people who are arguing on any topic that is not related to you. You cannot be the referee for others at your workplace! That is surely not your job.

To win and to grow in all the areas at your workplace, you never should have to cross your professional line of control.

Being over-friendly with your colleagues or being overanxious on matters that do not involve you, these are the types of things that ought to be avoided at your workplace, as too much of anything isn't good for anyone.

It is good to be friendly and to have the strongest positive AB quotient, to support everyone in need, to learn and to help others learn but suggestions that can go against one of the parties should be strictly avoided.

Who knows, maybe after 3-4 years Mr. smith role gets matured and he has now been promoted to as Team lead where both Nitesh and Akshay will be reporting to him. Now even if Akshay performs good, Nitesh's spirit will always remain low and negative on thinking about the past incident where Mr. smith supported Akshay or vice versa.

This may appear a very small and basic discussion point here but a very effective element that can save you from having any hindrance in your own career.

Maybe because of this misunderstanding about Mr. Smith, either of the team members will not be able to perform well, maybe Nitesh might not be able to respect Mr smith as a leader, maybe Nitesh would always go against the decisions of Mr. Smith's as according to him Mr. Smith is partial.

Mr. Smith must know that he himself is responsible for this situation in front of him, as he could have avoided getting into this argument in the first place. He could have left the coffee table, providing Akshay & Nitesh complete space to sort out their differences.

Save your energy and your potential both!

On the personal front, maybe Mr. Smith may have literally supported his best friend Akshay, it may not have mattered to Mr. Smith if Akshay was right or wrong.

If we go by logic, **we never ever should support the wrong person, whether it be at a personal or professional level, because the approach should be the same at both the places!**

I am leaving this decision up to you, which approach would you like to take in your personal life, keeping it in mind that the right way is to always support the truth.

If I imagine myself in this scenario and get stuck in a situation like this, I know I cannot escape the situation without giving an answer!

I would be honest in my answer and surely will try to give the answer that supports none!

My answer to my friend will be clear that *"yes you always share the required data with me but how can I speak in place of you, as I do not have a clear understanding as to what is causing Akshay to speak against you. Maybe you both need to sit down calmly and try to understand each other's point of view"*. This is the only diplomatic answer one can think of, that neither supports anyone, nor you are leaving the question unanswered and this indirectly respects the point highlighted by Nitesh. As such, both need to sort this out by themselves alone.

Be wise, and better not to get stuck in an awkward situation where you need to be partial or unfair with anyone. **This should never mean that a topic that involves you deserves your silence! You need to speak up if you are questioned by someone, considering that question must be related to you.**

Success Principle 17

A balance between What you earn & How you spend!

In this very important section, we are not going to learn much about how to save money through various schemes & policies, which alone is a huge topic, but here we will be focusing on how money saving is important to enjoy the fruits of SUCCESS consistently and forever.

When Success shake hands

When success will shake hands with you, you will get the required promotion, higher income, stability in career, respect, wisdom and most importantly, peace & harmony.

Do not ever forget the base from where you started, as the roots must remain as strong as the tree itself and sometimes too much success brings pride and ego. Apart from the money that you will earn during your success, the knowledge that you gain from your day-to-day experiences is also very precious. What you earned here is knowledge, skills, the power within you and your true self. **The wise decision would be to spend these intangible earnings to make the world better each day.**

Spend this knowledge and share with others, who need it the most, the more you spend this intangible earning (skills, experiences, positive energy etc.) the more it grows!

Previous Earnings Vs New Earnings

If you understood the SKILL DEVELOPMENT principle, then it will be easy for you to earn a salary that satisfies you mentally and is offered to you as per market trends and requirements. I want you to believe in the fact that your earnings can increase in 3 to 6 months or during your upcoming appraisal right after you upgraded your skill or got a certification.

I also told you about the constantly changing trends and that whatever we learn today will become an old version of itself in future, which means after every 2 years or 3 years (or as per specific industry after every 5 years) **you need upgradation in your skills, and this will be your investment in learning.**

Now, what happens when your salary increases let us say from 30,000/- INR per month to 50,000/- INR after doing a certified course or training which added value to your job profile. Imagine your expenditure is more and Savings are ZERO. You thought that from the time you start making 50,000/- per month, the hike of this 20 thousand will help you save some money. But to your surprise, with increasing salary, the banks now offered you 3 more credit cards & there are so many irresistible offers on online stores.

We plan our expenditures within whatever salary we get, but as soon as the salary increases, we never realise how & when our expenditures increase too. This may not be the case with all of us, but yes mostly this happens, the more the salary, the longer is our list of additional expenditures.

You got an amazing hike which is usually not given to most of the employees, but since you enhanced your skills, the employer knows that you are more valuable to them now, and if your goal & skills can be aligned with the company's vision then they surely would like to retain you & pay you.

No Saving! No Equilibrium!

Let us jump into a scenario very quickly: Imagine it just as a hypothetical situation, nothing more.

To maintain this equilibrium of learning & growth, you had planned to enhance your skills after every 2 or 3 years as per the latest trends and demand of the market but wait! From where you will get the funds to pay the fee for this certification.

This certification can be completed after clearing **2 exams** that are very tough. Apart from its difficulty, you need to pay 25,000/- INR for one single exam, which means you require a minimum of 50,000/- INR just for attempting this exam once.

Now, as this will be a very rewarding certification, you will need to study hard and you are not sure how many attempts it will take to clear these exams. It is for sure that after the completion of this certified program, you will have more growth opportunities in front of you.

Maybe the organisation would like to mature your role and give you your own team to work with (leadership skills are to be gained by then), wherein as of now no one is reporting to you directly. So, this is the magic of skills development which offers you limitless opportunities.

It is good if your company is ready to sponsor 50% to 60% of the course fee, but then they have a bond that you cannot leave the organisation before 2 years or 3 years in return of this sponsorship. If in any case, you leave before the said duration, the sponsored amount will be recovered back from your salary. Now you are not sure if you would like to go ahead with the bond as you have some specific career plan laid out for yourself. Also, the company will pay this amount only for 1 single attempt, on failing to complete the certification once you are not getting the sponsorship again.

These conditions may vary from one organisation to another as different companies have different skill development sponsorship policies. If you are not aware of any such policies or sponsorships in your organisation, then you must check with your employer about the availability of any such policy or sponsorship program.

If you are at the early stages of your career and would like to go for a short-term course, certification or training, but are short of money. In such a case if your employer is ready to sponsor it fully or partially, **then you must not think a lot about bonds and its condition** as it is a normal trend in the industry to stay with a company for as long as possible in the initial years of your career. Take the sponsorship in this case & follow the guidelines mentioned in the bond. It is great if after this you find opportunities for yourself within the same organisation as this is the reason as to why the company is ready to sponsor your certification.

Now coming back to the scenario, after giving it a thought you decided not to take sponsorship from the company, as you have support from your family and they are ready to give you 50,000/- INR as of now to complete this certification, or maybe you have some old savings that you are ready to spend on your skill development considering the ROI (return on investment).

After you gave the exam, the result came out and guess what!

You passed one of the exams but failed to clear the other one and for that, you need to go for a second attempt.

Introspect as per the given scenario, will you be quitting here and waste the other 25 thousand INR also? Or you would like to go for the second attempt? If yes, then how?

You already used your savings; now you have no money; further, you do not really want to ask for more money from your family, as now you are independent and earn well.

Even if you try to cut down your expenditures after paying house rent, bills etc. then also saving will be around 5 to 7 thousand INR approximately in a month, that means you need to wait for 3-4 months to save 25 thousand INR. As per one of the conditions, there is a time limitation as well, that you need to re-attempt your exam within 40 days from the date of the result.

Such a stressful situation! Isn't it? I agree; it is. But now the **rotation of investment** will come into play, let us see how?

Proactive Approach: 17A

Rotation of Investment

For increasing the Savings & the Skills simultaneously.

The time that you got a good salary hike because of your hard work and skill upgradation that is the time you **focus on not increasing your expenditure at all**, just keep managing your expenditure the way you were doing in the past, at least for the next 6 to 7 months. Whatever appraised amount you get now, without giving it even a 2nd thought, just save it in some other bank account and make sure not to use those savings.

For example, we had discussed an increase of 20,000 /- INR per month in your salary, i.e. your salary revised from 30,000/- to 50,000/- INR. If you really do not increase your expenditures, then now with this increased salary you would be able to save between 18 to 20 thousand INR every month. Within the next 2 months, you will be able to save almost 36 to 40 thousand INR and in a year your total saving will be somewhere between 2 lakhs to 2.5 lakhs.

How the rotation of this investment (i.e. savings) can be done for skill enhancement after a certain period of time:

It is very simple, you use the required money from this savings to develop your skills and as per the above scenario to give yourself a chance to clear the exam. It is ok that you were not able to clear it in a single attempt. **We previously did learn as to what should be our next step when encountering any such failure, i.e. we bounce back again & again until we get it right** (as per Bounce Back Transformation Model: 13B). With this positive attitude, we would clear the exam in maybe the 2nd or 3rd attempt, but surely we will do it!

Practically speaking, in this situation where the money is involved, bouncing back will not be sufficient, you need to have some savings in your bank account too. The money you have saved is the investment for your own career growth. Using these savings cum investment at required intervals, you can develop your skills from time to time and it will have the best ROI (return of investment).

Now you have cleared both the exams, you became a certified coach, or certified Sr. project manager or a certified Sr. technical architect etc. What happens next is no surprise. You will be rewarded as per the skills you have developed whether in this organisation or in any other organisation just in case if you are overqualified now as per company's work requirements.

Rotation will start when you keep on increasing your savings for "Skill development" and utilise it in every 2- 3 years in order to make maximum use of the "OBCD long-term career planner" that you had read about in earlier section. As you begin to rise-up in ranks and reach a senior profile like a General manager, Deputy manager, or Sr. design head etc., **your savings bracket expands automatically due to the increase in salary associated with these profiles.**

Your salary now increases from 50,000/- INR per month to let us say 70 to 80,000/- INR, and then from 80,000/- INR to 1 lakh/2 lakhs as you go higher in the hierarchy. You still should save for skill development, **but only a little will now be required for it as you have saved enough and witnessed the magic of ROI done in this particular area.**

Envision your life after 10 to 15 years of your career as per OBCD planner and after **yearly rotation on this skill-based investment,** you reach up to a level where you monitor most of the work and guide the teams to work hard. Your efforts would then be measured through the ways you foster your subordinates as a good leader. A good leader who not only sits and orders but puts all his efforts to foster his/her subordinates to become the future leaders of the world.

As now you are getting such a satisfactory high salary due to which now your savings bracket has expanded vastly and you have started to invest in financial markets, in fixed deposits, medical insurances, properties, Mutual funds etc. Now, this second part of the investment is part of your personal life & it's completely up to you as to how you would like to **plan these 2nd type of investments that are not related to skill development.** The 2nd type of investment is also very important & you must start checking upon this 2nd type of savings side by side.

This scenario ends here, I did not pick an imaginary character this time for this specific scenario like Mr Rajat, Smith, Jackson etc. but I intentionally portrayed you in this last scenario and I am sure you understood the purpose of it. This way, for a few minutes we imagined our future self and imagined us being at a higher profile or as a future leader based on the skills and smarter hard work to achieve success on their career map.

Proactive Approach: 17B

Quick tips that will help you "save money" easily:

Prepare a simple budget sheet for yourself after all necessary expenditures figure out the "not so necessary" expenditures that are refraining you from saving money.

Understand the difference between your "NEED" and your "WANT":

- **Need is unavoidable expenses** like house rent, bills, food expenses etc.

- **Want is an avoidable expense,** use of credit cards unnecessarily to buy things and then paying the banks a good interest in return, or expenditure done on parties, shopping, trips, gifts etc. These "wants" are surely important and part of your life, but you should spend on these wisely after **locking some specific amount from your salary as your "savings".**

Lock Your "Savings" First!

I have created a sample budget sheet of an employee whose salary is 50,000/- INR per month.

The before & after the budget sheet will help us save some money if, in the past, we were not able to do so.

This is to be considered just as a sample and this budget sheet can vary from person to person depending upon their personal needs & expenditure.

The purpose is to understand the procedure to fix or lock a certain percentage from our salary as savings at the start of the month. After a year of regular monthly saving, make sure to either invest these funds for your skill development (highly recommended) or keep on adding an amount to this saving on a yearly basis. To do the savings effectively your saving percentage should at least increase by 4% to 5% every year, or more, depending upon your appraised CTC for that year.

You can fix or lock as much percentage as you want to save monthly depending upon your expenditures.

At the least, your monthly savings should be somewhere around 15 to 16% of your net salary, i.e. your take-home salary.

Basic budget sheet

Budget sheet before locking the Savings

Salary: 50,000/- INR	Any other income: 0	Total income: 50000/-INR
Expenses	**Utilized**	**Balance**
(1-5 are "Need" expenses)		50000
1. Groceries	5000.00 INR	45000.00
2. Utility bills	5000.00 INR	40000.00
3. EMI's /loan	7000.00 INR	33000.00
4. House Rent	15000.00 INR	18000.00
5. Medical/misc.	5000.00 INR	13000.00
(6th one is a "Want" expenses)		
6. Others – shopping, parties, gifting etc.	7000.00 INR	6000.00
		These 6000/- INR is the left-over amount after meeting our "NEED" & "WANT" expenses both, last month maybe it was 2 thousand and before that could even be zero, this is a non-recordable expense)
	Total Leftover	6000.00

This simple format will work fine; you just need to work on it once and then it gets imprinted in your mind for the rest of the months. Savings should be fixed and should be kept in some separate bank account only.

As per 2nd budget sheet, where we have fixed & locked the SAVINGS amount which is 15% to 16% (at the minimum) of the net salary, we were able to save 96,000/- INR by the end of the year. You can lock as much as you want as your savings, this is just an example.

Success Principle 18

You, as a Powerhouse

Do you believe in "powers" and "energies" of the Universe? If not, **then start believing & you will see the magic happening in your life**. Read this section more like a "HUMAN" rather than just a "resource" of any organisation, as this one approach will change not only your professional existence but also your existence on earth as a Human being!

There exists a surreal **Power** within you that can only be experienced with a distinct frame of mind.

If you want to open the gates for growth, success, stability, and prosperity in your life, then try to **make yourself a living powerhouse!**

Congratulations, as by now, you have understood so many concepts and tricks that will not only make you an extraordinary person at the workplace but also an extraordinary Human being in your personal life.

I have kept this section in the last part of the book because after going through all these concepts & principles, this last technique will become **your partner for life & will be the quickest & fastest way to achieve your goal.**

We have a lot of distractions, disturbances in personal life that literally have an impact on our professional life. Work-Life Balance can be maintained with this power that lies dormant within you. You can clearly understand the purpose of your life by digging out this best version that is hidden in you.

How does it really work?

With this technique, you will wake someone from inside of you and this "extraordinary someone" becomes the powerhouse to deal with come what may!

With correct maintenance of this powerhouse, you will be able to induce the heightened intuitive life state that is awake, focussed and experiences no disturbance.

Developing a heightened state for concentration, focus and attentiveness

Have you heard of people increasing their focus & concentration through meditation? I can tell you that this surely works wonders.

Remember the **Alpha state of mind** to start our first 30 minutes of the day. It will be good if you do this daily and it will be great if you do the same while going to bed. It is easy when we lie on the bed either focus on our breathing, or listen to affirmations; you can also chant a mantra, or focus on 7 chakras balancing etc.

It really does not matter which technique or which meditative process you like, **the destination & result will likely be the same as all these techniques activate and awaken your intuitive side** and you become more focussed and automatically gain clarity on the things you have to do.

Where does this powerhouse get its energy from?

The answer is simple - it gets the energy **From the Universe.**

If you never believed it before, then please, try it once and your body & mind will get energised every day. Your mind will become more focussed and you will perform with your highest potential, be it your personal life or professional life!

This cannot be understood by scenarios or by reading hypothetical situations like the rest of the sections. **To feel this power that was always there within you, you must dive deep into your mind** & during this process, you will find an "extraordinary you". This **extraordinary "you" pull energy directly from the Universe during meditation and then the divine magic begins!**

When you align yourself with the powers of the Universe, your mind, body & soul starts sending relevant signals during day-to-day activities you do. As an advantage, it increases your decision-making ability, and your heart & mind can sense which decision is better for you at each step of your career and in personal life.

If you were already doing something like this, then it's wonderful, if not then you must start with guided meditation videos for at least a week and see the magic unravel!

I personally find guided meditation much easier than the meditation we try to do alone. It supports us and protects us from any distractions.

No meditative technique will suit you until you try it once

wholeheartedly. *It is like picking up candy from a box containing different flavours and while doing so again and again suddenly you discover that one candy which tastes the best according to you, and now you will always prefer eating only that.*

You need to find the best suitable meditative technique out of hundreds of techniques. For this, you need to keep practising until you find the best fit for your soul & mind.

Do not worry whichever religion you are from or in whichever country you are staying in; **the power will surely reach you if you follow the technique correctly.**

Meditation is not a restriction; it is "Freedom."

Meditation is not a restriction that forces you to sit silently & that it demands to focus on self; it is the "Freedom". The freedom of Soul, Heart & Mind from every boundary, pain, curse, sorrow and failure.

- Shivali Tandon

Meditation, for me, is not about imprisoning oneself within any boundary or restriction or forcing oneself to sit for hours and hours in order to build better focus and concentration. **You will never get the required result from such forcible meditation practice.**

Meditation is the way **to find a connection between our Soul and this Universe. Meditation is FREEDOM,** i.e. our soul becomes free from every boundary, limitation, pain, curse, sorrow and failure, and it begins to fly higher & higher to directly align itself with the energies of the Universe, and as a result of that, **we become a powerhouse to exhibit our highest potential.**

To understand it in very easy terms, I would like to share the meaning of "meditation" shared by Yongey Mingyur Rinpoche, a Tibetan teacher who in one of his sessions explain that Mediation is "Awareness". When we meditate, we focus on our pain, happiness, success, failure & hardships that create awareness towards it and that is "meditation".

You will try many techniques as YouTube & google is full of extensive information regarding hundreds of meditative techniques, starting from beginners to advanced level, but pick the one which is best suited for you.

It is always better to start with guided meditation or with simple breathing techniques as a beginner. **This experience will give you so much of joy & power that I can't explain it here in words, and a time will come when naturally your soul will start demanding more of this joy & power. Ultimately, you will develop your own technique to connect instantly with the Universe.**

A couple of techniques I use to recharge myself (powerhouse) are:

1. For me, **7 chakras balancing is** a way to balance major elements of my life; it covers everything which is imbalanced internally and externally. By this guided practise, you can convert all your weaknesses into your strength. After consistent practise, you can notice drastic changes in your physical, mental, emotional and spiritual wellbeing.

2. Putting on earphones and hearing soft meditative music (available online) and simultaneously **focusing on my breathing helps me find the purest form of my existence.** I love to explore this extraordinary experience of mind & soul together. I make sure to do this with earphones/headphones "On" as it saves me from any distraction & disturbance that can occur due to sounds/noise we hear in our surroundings.
3. **Chanting mantras** are another way that I practice sometimes when I feel low and doubtful.

"I cannot tell you which technique will be best for you. You will have to find your own technique, that is the only best way to really experience **the magic of cosmic energy that is there in the Universe."**

Almost all your problems will have relevant solutions if you start practising this last exercise on a daily basis. I know it seems tough but start with just 5 minutes of focusing on your breathing while hearing a very soft calming meditation music with earphones on.

I am sharing this with my own experience that after correct and consistent practice, you literally will become a Powerhouse! This will be the most extraordinary change you will ever notice in yourself.

If you are a beginner or want to explore a couple of techniques, please go ahead & start your search using these keywords:

- Power of positive thinking
- How affirmations work in real life
- Listen to the affirmations video related to success, money &

abundance, career, concentration & growth. There are hundreds of affirmation videos online, pick your favourite ones and allow your brain to absorb these affirmations.

- Write these affirmations daily if possible, for best results.
- Guided meditation.
- Meditation techniques for increasing focus & concentration.
- Guided meditation for developing the highest work potential.
- What role do 7 Chakras play in Human body?
- How to balance 7 Chakras & what are the benefits.
- 7 chakras guided meditation.

Your search can go beyond these keywords; it is like drinking the nectar of joy, peace & transformation. **The more you drink it, the more powerful you become.**

The benefit is not only restricted to feeling the divine magic, but you can witness visible results too at your workplace & in personal life as you expand your life as an extraordinary Human being.

Correct use of this Power!

Do not forget the principle of "CAUSE & EFFECT" we read earlier (Proactive Approach: 9A). You cannot become a powerhouse if you just meditate for yourself and absorb the powers from the Universe and in return, you hurt someone or have a negative AB quotient towards your life. **If your actions do not really resonate with what you feel inside, then this power is of no use!**

Your actions should reflect happiness and when you spread this positive power in your surrounding, you create a "CAUSE". In the same way, whatever "CAUSES" we create with our actions become the "EFFECT" of it. So these two terms are related to each other as to whatever "causes" we create today brings an equivalent "effect" in our lives.

Change of approach is a journey to transform ourselves into an extraordinary human being who has the powerful potential to transform him/herself into an extraordinary employee at the workplace as well.

Apart from being an author of this book, I am a human being who truly believes in God and in the energy of this Universe, I send my prayers to all my readers. I hope that you all will be able to make an extraordinary difference in your life and **may this book become your best friend during crucial times and that you are able to refer to these scenarios and exercises at the times of need.**

My purpose of writing this book for you all is simple. One is that I wanted to live my dream and passion, also to dig out the better version within me and this is one step towards it. Secondly, I wanted to follow the guidance given by Mr. Naveen Jain that our success is justified only when we are able to improve someone else's life through it. I am sure without any doubt that by the end of this book, your way of thinking has been renewed and your approach of looking at life & success will also get changed with time & real-time experiences.

The only thing which is required, and you must do **is to make honest efforts each day** based upon these success principles, and do not restrict yourself only to this book. You can keep on enhancing your knowledge. You need to be sure which all sources you are using to learn all these things. Always check if the given information is valid and relevant as you can be misguided by a lot of wrong information and courses that demand money to make you extraordinary. **You must believe in yourself and your potential, and that you cannot become extraordinary by just paying money**, this is an **internal process involving mind & heart** which can first be achieved through strong determination and wisdom. Always use authentic platforms to get correct guidance related to life transformation, success and abundance.

I wish you all good luck!

Let's connect for any questions or suggestions if you have.

Derive maximum benefit from these Success Principles models, proactive approaches & activities that are mentioned in the book! For ease of access, I have labelled a few important ones for you in the index below, so that you can refer the same anytime anywhere as per need.

www.ingramcontent.com/pod-product-compliance
Lightning Source LLC
Chambersburg PA
CBHW062103160726
48282CB00026B/648
* 9 7 8 9 3 9 0 6 6 1 0 3 9 *